ARBITRARY BORDERS

Political Boundaries in World History

The Division of the Middle East
The Treaty of Sèvres

The Iron Curtain
The Cold War in Europe

The Mason–Dixon Line

Vietnam: The 17th Parallel

Korea: The 38th Parallel

The U.S.–Mexico Border
The Treaty of Guadalupe Hidalgo

Europe, 1948–1989

Communist countries

Non-communist countries

"Iron Curtain"

ATLANTIC
OCEAN

SWEDEN

FINLAND

NORWAY

North
Sea

Baltic
Sea

DENMARK

IRELAND

SOVIET
UNION

GREAT
BRITAIN

NETHERLANDS

EAST
GERMANY

POLAND

BELGIUM

LUXEMBOURG

WEST
GERMANY

CZECHOSLOVAKIA

AUSTRIA

HUNGARY

SWITZERLAND

ROMANIA

FRANCE

YUGOSLAVIA

Black
Sea

Adriatic Sea

ITALY

BULGARIA

PORTUGAL

ALBANIA

SPAIN

GREECE

TURKEY

Mediterranean Sea

AFRICA

ARBITRARY BORDERS

Political Boundaries in World History

The Iron Curtain
The Cold War in Europe

Bruce L. Brager

Foreword by
Senator **George J. Mitchell**

Introduction by
James I. Matray
California State University, Chico

CHELSEA HOUSE
PUBLISHERS
A Haights Cross Communications Company

Philadelphia

FRONTIS The approximate location of the Iron Curtain is shown on a map of Western and Eastern Europe.

CHELSEA HOUSE PUBLISHERS

VP, NEW PRODUCT DEVELOPMENT   Sally Cheney
DIRECTOR OF PRODUCTION   Kim Shinners
CREATIVE MANAGER Takeshi Takahashi
MANUFACTURING MANAGER Diann Grasse

Staff for THE IRON CURTAIN

EXECUTIVE EDITOR Lee Marcott
PRODUCTION EDITOR Megan Emery
ASSISTANT PHOTO EDITOR Noelle Nardone
INTERIOR DESIGN Keith Trego
COVER DESIGNER Keith Trego
LAYOUT EJB Publishing Services

www.chelseahouse.com

First Printing

1 3 5 7 9 8 6 4 2

Library of Congress Cataloging-in-Publication Data
Brager, Bruce L., 1949–
   The Iron Curtain : the Cold War in Europe / by Bruce L. Brager.
      v. cm. — (Arbitrary borders)
Contents: Let them come to Berlin — The Soviet perspective — The American perspective — 1948 : Berlin — 1961 : Berlin again — Entangling alliances — Interrelationships, Hungary and Suez — The short Prague spring — 1989 : the end of an era. includes bibliographical references and index. 1. Cold War — Juvenile literature. 2. Communist strategy — Juvenile literature. 3. Berlin Wall, Berlin, Germany, 1961–1989 — Juvenile literature. 4. Soviet Union — Foreign relations — United States — Juvenile literature. 5. Unoted States — Foreign relations — Soviet Union — Juvenile literature. [1. Cold War. 2. Soviet Union — Foreign relations — United States. 3. United States — Foreign relations — Soviet Union.] I. Title. II. Series.
D843.B658 2003 940.55—dc   2003023454

ISBN: 0-7910-7832-9

Contents

Foreword

Senator **George J. Mitchell**

I spent years working for peace in Northern Ireland and in the Middle East. I also made many visits to the Balkans during the long and violent conflict there.

Each of the three areas is unique; so is each conflict. But there are also some similarities: in each, there are differences over religion, national identity, and territory.

Deep religious differences that lead to murderous hostility are common in human history. Competing aspirations involving national identity are more recent occurrences, but often have been just as deadly.

Territorial disputes—two or more people claiming the same land—are as old as humankind. Almost without exception, such disputes have been a factor in recent conflicts. It is impossible to calculate the extent to which the demand for land—as opposed to religion, national identity, or other factors— figures in the motivation of people caught up in conflict. In my experience it is a substantial factor that has played a role in each of the three conflicts mentioned above.

In Northern Ireland and the Middle East, the location of the border was a major factor in igniting and sustaining the conflict. And it is memorialized in a dramatic and visible way: through the construction of large walls whose purpose is to physically separate the two communities.

In Belfast, the capital and largest city in Northern Ireland, the so-called "Peace Line" cuts through the heart of the city, right across urban streets. Up to thirty feet high in places, topped with barbed wire in others, it is an ugly reminder of the duration and intensity of the conflict.

In the Middle East, as I write these words, the government of Israel has embarked on a huge and controversial effort to construct a security fence roughly along the line that separates Israel from the West Bank.

Having served a tour of duty with the U.S. Army in Berlin, which was once the site of the best known of modern walls, I am skeptical of their long-term value, although they often serve short-term needs. But it cannot be said that such structures represent a new idea. Ancient China built the Great Wall to deter nomadic Mongol tribes from attacking its population.

In much the same way, other early societies established boundaries and fortified them militarily to achieve the goal of self-protection. Borders always have separated people. Indeed, that is their purpose.

This series of books examines the important and timely issue of the significance of arbitrary borders in history. Each volume focuses attention on a territorial division, but the analytical approach is more comprehensive. These studies describe arbitrary borders as places where people interact differently from the way they would if the boundary did not exist. This pattern is especially pronounced where there is no geographic reason for the boundary and no history recognizing its legitimacy. Even though many borders have been defined without legal precision, governments frequently have provided vigorous monitoring and military defense for them.

This series will show how the migration of people and exchange of goods almost always work to undermine the separation that borders seek to maintain. The continuing evolution of a European community provides a contemporary example illustrating this point, most obviously with the adoption of a single currency. Moreover, even former Soviet bloc nations have eliminated barriers to economic and political integration.

Globalization has emerged as one of the most powerful forces in international affairs during the twenty-first century. Not only have markets for the exchange of goods and services become genuinely worldwide, but instant communication and sharing of information have shattered old barriers separating people. Some scholars even argue that globalization has made the entire concept of a territorial nation-state irrelevant. Although the assertion is certainly premature and probably wrong, it highlights the importance of recognizing how borders often have reflected and affirmed the cultural, ethnic, or linguistic perimeters that define a people or a country.

Since the Cold War ended, competition over resources or a variety of interests threaten boundaries more than ever, resulting in contentious interaction, conflict, adaptation, and intermixture. How people define their borders is also a factor in determining how events develop in the surrounding region. This series will provide detailed descriptions of selected arbitrary borders in history with the objective of providing insights on how artificial boundaries separating people will influence international affairs during the next century.

Senator George J. Mitchell
October 2003

Introduction

James I. Matray
California State University, Chico

Throughout history, borders have separated people. Scholars have devoted considerable attention to assessing the significance and impact of territorial boundaries on the course of human history, explaining how they often have been sources of controversy and conflict. In the modern age, the rise of nation-states in Europe created the need for governments to negotiate treaties to confirm boundary lines that periodically changed as a consequence of wars and revolutions. European expansion in the nineteenth century imposed new borders on Africa and Asia. Many native peoples viewed these boundaries as arbitrary and, after independence, continued to contest their legitimacy. At the end of both world wars in the twentieth century, world leaders drew artificial and impermanent lines separating assorted people around the globe. Borders certainly are among the most important factors that have influenced the development of world affairs.

Chelsea House Publishers decided to publish a collection of books looking at arbitrary borders in history in response to the revival of the nuclear crisis in North Korea in October 2002. Recent tensions on the Korean peninsula are a direct consequence of the partitioning of Korea at the 38th parallel after World War II. Other nations in the course of human history have suffered due to similar artificial divisions. The reasons for establishing arbitrary borders have differed, but usually arise from either domestic or international factors and are often a combination of both. In the case of Korea, it was the United States and the Soviet Union who decided in August 1945 to partition the country at the 38th parallel. Ostensibly, the purpose was to facilitate the acceptance of the surrender of Japanese forces at the end of World War II. However, historians have presented persuasive evidence that a political contest existed inside Korea to decide the future of the nation after forty years of Japanese colonial rule. Therefore, Korea's division at the 38th parallel was an artificial boundary that symbolized the split among the Korean people about the nation's destiny. On the right were conservative landowners who had closely aligned with the Japanese, many of whom were outright collaborators. On the left, there were far more individuals who favored revolutionary change. In fact, Communists provided the leadership and direction for the independence movement inside Korea from the 1920s until the end of World War II. After 1945, two Koreas emerged that reflected these divergent ideologies. But the Korean people have never accepted the legitimacy or permanence of the division imposed by foreign powers.

Korea's experience in dealing with the artificial division of its country may well be unique, but it is not without historical parallels. The first set of books in this series on arbitrary borders examines six key chapters in human history. One volume will look at the history of the 38th parallel in Korea. Other volumes will provide description and analysis of the division of the Middle East after World War I; the Cold War as symbolized by the Iron Curtain in Central Europe; the United States.-Mexico Border; the 17th parallel in Vietnam, and the Mason-Dixon Line. Future books will address the Great Wall in China, Northern Ireland's border, and the Green Line in Israel. Admittedly, there are many significant differences between these boundaries, but these books will cover as many common themes as possible. In so doing, each will help readers conceptualize how factors such as colonialism, culture, and economics determine the nature of contact between people along these borders. Although globalization has emerged as a powerful force working against the creation and maintenance of lines separating people, boundaries are not likely to disappear as factors with a continuing influence on world events. This series of books will provide insights about the impact of arbitrary borders on human history and how such borders continue to shape the modern world.

James I. Matray
Chico, California
November 2003

"From Stettin in the Baltic to Trieste in the Adriatic, an iron curtain has descended across the Continent."

—Winston Churchill, March 5, 1946[1]

"Due to the situation which has evolved as a result of the formation of the Commonwealth of Independent States, I hereby discontinue my activities at the post of President of the Union of Soviet Socialist Republics."

—Mikhail Gorbachev, December 25, 1991[2]

1

"Let Them Come to Berlin"

Visiting Central Europe, about 1962, the visitor would not see a real "iron curtain." There was no huge piece of grim drapery splitting Europe between Communist dictatorships and democracies. A curtain can be removed easily, an iron curtain cannot. A curtain temporarily shuts off one area from another. An iron curtain symbolically represents an attempt to permanently, artificially, and arbitrarily split off an area from its neighbors.

Such an arbitrary border, frequently imposed by outside powers, directly and indirectly affects the lives of the people on both sides. Day-to-day social contacts between people on the two sides of the border can suddenly be cut off. Economic contacts, perhaps those under way for centuries, can be severed abruptly or continued only under strictly regulated conditions. The effects of such a border, in particular that in Europe, can be felt worldwide. An arbitrary border can bring peace to a war-torn area, but at the risk of a far greater war than had been seen before. Perversely, this very risk can bring peace, by raising the stakes if a war starts to escalate to unacceptable levels.

A curtain, even one made of iron, might have added just a bit of decoration, might have added to the quality of the scenery. There was no iron curtain, but there was a lot of steel—barbed wire, ground radar, watchtowers, machine guns in the hands of soldiers willing to use them. One could tell where democracy ended and totalitarianism began, on borders extending from the Arctic Circle almost to the Mediterranean Sea.

The "Iron Curtain," a phrase introduced to the public in a speech by former British Prime Minister Winston Churchill in 1946, represented the European part of the "Cold War," the generally peaceful but highly dangerous 45-year competition between the United States and its allies and the Soviet Union and its allies. "Central Front" was also applied to the European theater of the Cold War, a deliberate use of a military term applied perhaps not in expectation but in fear that the Cold War would become hot.

The Iron Curtain, symbolic though it was, had a geographic center: West Berlin. Since the end of World War II, by agreement among the major allies fighting Nazi Germany—United States, Great Britain, and the Soviet Union—the United States, Great Britain, and France had occupied West Berlin. West Berlin had a democratically elected mayor. Despite Soviet protests, and despite an official status summarized in a 1971 treaty as "not a constituent part of the Federal Republic of Germany and not governed by it,"[3] West Berlin was effectively part of West Germany.

Beginning in 1961, West Berlin had a steel and concrete curtain surrounding it and cutting it off from East Berlin and East Germany, the country established from the Soviet zone of occupation of Germany. The wall had been intended to keep East Germans from fleeing to West Berlin and freedom. With a few exceptions, it did that. It also made a rather crude statement that Communist governments, running self-declared workers' paradises, did not trust their own people not to leave when they had the chance. The Berlin Wall declared that freedom was too much of a temptation; that even an official, if arbitrary and artificial, border was not enough. A real, visible, physical wall was necessary.

One of the central events of the Cold War occurred on June 26, 1963, about halfway through the Cold War, just a few feet from the Berlin Wall. At this time, at least the tense standoff between the two superpowers had eased off from the Cuban Missile Crisis of October 1962. The ill-advised Soviet placement of offensive nuclear weapons in Cuba, 90 miles from the southern tip of the United States, had come within hours, or less, of touching off a nuclear war. By June 1963, both sides had pulled back from that highly dangerous brink. The treaty banning nuclear weapons testing in the atmosphere, the first such treaty between the Soviet Union and the United States, was being negotiated. Military tensions were easing.

The arbitrary border called the Iron Curtain, however, remained as strong as ever. Europe was still split, with contacts

Shortly after the end of World War II, Winston Churchill toured the United States with President Harry Truman. On receiving an honorary degree at Westminster College in Missouri, Churchill coined the phrase the "Iron Curtain" during a speech in which he warned of the dangers of communism.

between the sections limited. Eastern Europe was not free, continuing under the tight control of the Soviets. The Berlin Wall stood. American President John F. Kennedy, visiting Europe, had come for a brief trip to Berlin to show continued American support for West Germany and for Berlin. Kennedy spoke, within sight of the wall, to a crowd of at least one million people (60 percent of West Berlin's population at the time) about what West Berlin meant to the free world. As Kennedy spoke, a real curtain, large and red, made of cloth, hung on the

Brandenburg Gate, the ceremonial center of the old United Berlin, just inside East Berlin. The curtain, as was intended, blocked Kennedy's view into East Berlin, and East Berliners' view of him.

The climax of Kennedy's speech is what is remembered about that day. The climax was particularly dramatic, even for a president known for dramatic speeches:

> There are many people in the world who really don't understand, or say they don't, what is the great issue between the free world and the Communist world. Let them come to Berlin. There are some who say that Communism is the wave of the future. Let them come to Berlin... and there are even a few who say that it is true that Communism is an evil system, but it permits us to make economic progress, "Lasst sie nach Berlin Kommen."
>
> Freedom has many difficulties and democracy is not perfect, but we have never had to put a wall up to keep our people in ....
>
> We ... look forward to the day when this city will be joined as one—and this country, and this great continent of Europe—in a peaceful and hopeful globe. When that day finally comes, as it will, the people of West Berlin can take sober satisfaction in the fact that they were in the front lines for almost two decades.
>
> All free men, wherever they may live, are citizens of Berlin, and, therefore, as a free man, I take pride in the words "*Ich bin ein Berliner.*"[4]

Because of a slight error in translation, Kennedy actually said he was a pastry, *ein Berliner.* A citizen of Berlin was *Berliner.* The Germans, however, certainly knew what he meant. Kennedy speech writer Theodore Sorenson, who probably wrote the speech, later wrote that "The West Berliners ... gave John Kennedy the most overwhelming reception of his career."[5]

In 1963, American president John F. Kennedy came to Berlin to show support for West Germany and Berlin. This visit to the wall was the president's first look at the Cold War dividing line. In this photograph, President Kennedy stands on a platform, the fourth man from the right, overlooking the wall. He addressed about one million people in West Berlin. The curtain behind the Brandenburg Gate in the background was put up by the East German government to prevent anyone listening in East Berlin from actually seeing Kennedy.

FAVORABLE REFERENCES TO THE DEVIL

People of Kennedy's and Sorenson's generation probably recognized the irony that Berlin had become a symbol of freedom and resistance to expansionist tyranny at the height of the Cold War. Though never the ideological center of Nazi Germany—that dubious honor belonged to Munich and Nuremberg—30 years before, Berlin was the center of government, the control center of the greatest threat to freedom and security the world has known. Aside from the Jews, for whom Nazi leader Adolf Hitler had a pathological hatred, Communism was Hitler's main target.

Communism was both different from and a rival to Nazism. Both systems were threats to the democratic West. However, as soon as he learned of the June 22, 1941, massive German invasion of the Soviet Union, British Prime Minister Winston Churchill, a bitter foe of Communism, declared, "If Hitler invaded Hell I would at least make a favorable reference to the Devil in the House of Commons."[6] The United States, still not at war, expanded its program of aid, already providing vital assistance to Great Britain, to include the Soviet Union. Six months later, after the Japanese attack on Pearl Harbor brought the United States into the war, formal military cooperation began.

SELECTION FROM REPORT OF THE CRIMEA CONFERENCE DECLARATION ON LIBERATED EUROPE

... The establishment of order in Europe and the rebuilding of national economic life must be achieved by processes which will enable the liberated peoples to destroy the last vestiges of Nazism and Fascism and to create democratic institutions of their own choice. This is a principle of the Atlantic Charter—the right of all peoples to choose the form of government under which they will live—the restoration of sovereign rights and self-government to those peoples who have been forcibly deprived of them by the aggressor nations.

To foster the conditions in which the liberated peoples may exercise these rights, the three governments will jointly assist the people in any European liberated state or former Axis satellite state in Europe where in their judgment conditions require (a) to establish conditions of internal peace; (b) to carry out emergency measures for the relief of distressed people; (c) to form interim governmental authorities broadly representative of all democratic elements in the population and pledged to the earliest possible establishment through free elections of governments responsive to the will of the people; and (d) to facilitate where necessary the holding of such elections.

Source: U.S. Department of State, *Foreign Relations of the United States, Diplomatic Papers, The Conferences at Malta and Yalta*, 1945. Washington, D.C.: United States Government Printing Office, 1955, p. 972.

The Soviet Union never became part of the close military partnership formed between Great Britain and the United States, including the unified Combined Chiefs of Staff controlling both nations' military forces. There was strategic coordination, starting with Stalin's urgings for the British and Americans to open a second front in Europe. Stalin also agreed that, once Germany was defeated, the Soviet Union would enter the war against Japan.

For the first few years of the partnership, political as well as military harmony seemed to prevail. The August 1941 Atlantic Charter informal agreements between Roosevelt and Churchill supported the idea of no forced territorial changes and the rights of people to choose their own governments. In January 1942 these were formalized in the United Nations Declaration, which the "Big Three" (Roosevelt, Churchill, and Stalin) and representatives of 22 other nations signed. A similar agreement among the Big Three and China was signed in Moscow in October 1943.

By January 1945, the end of the war, at least in Europe, was close. The last German offensives of the war, the Battle of the Bulge and Operation Northwind, had been stopped and pushed back with heavy German casualties. The Soviets had begun their final push in the east. On February 4, 1945, Roosevelt, Churchill, and Stalin met at Yalta, a port on the Black Sea in the southern part of the Soviet Union.

YALTA

President Franklin D. Roosevelt was at sea on January 30, 1945, his sixty-third birthday. Various groups on board the American warship on which he was sailing presented him with a total of five birthday cakes. James F. Byrnes, director of the Office of War Mobilization and later secretary of state, asked Roosevelt's daughter if the President was well. Roosevelt's daughter and his doctor assured Byrnes that Roosevelt had a cold and a sinus infection but was otherwise fine. "Since he had so often 'bounced back' after an illness," Byrne wrote two years later, "I dismissed my fears."[7] Roosevelt looked better by the time the ship reached Malta, where he and his party would change to an airplane for the rest of the trip to Yalta, where the Big Three—Roosevelt, Churchill, and Stalin—would meet.

At Malta, Roosevelt flew for the first time in an airplane built for his personal use, nicknamed the *Sacred Cow*. The plane even had an elevator, to enable Roosevelt to enter the plane in his wheelchair. (Roosevelt was disabled with polio.

Byrnes later wrote about another concern. "So far as I could see, the President had made little preparation for the Yalta Conference. His inauguration had taken place the Saturday before we left and for ten days preceding that he had been overwhelmed with engagements."[8] Byrnes, White House Chief of Staff Admiral William D. Leahy, and Roosevelt had discussed some of the issues. Byrnes, however, learned at Malta that Roosevelt had an extensive file of studies and recommendations prepared by the State Department. He continued,

> Later, when I saw some of these splendid studies I greatly regretted that they had not been considered on board ship. I am sure the failure to study them while en route was due to the President's illness. And I am sure that only President Roosevelt, with his intimate knowledge of the problems, could have handled the situation so well with so little preparation.[9]

Roosevelt's chief confidant, Harry Hopkins, was also sick during the conference. Byrnes may be right that Roosevelt's lack of preparation did not hurt the conference, but one has to wonder if the health of the chief participant and of his chief aide played a role in the eventual results of the conference.

Roosevelt has been described as focusing too much on an idealistic peace, assuming that other nations would realize our goodwill and behave reasonably because this was the "right" thing to do. One historian has written, "Roosevelt had ignored almost entirely the fundamental problem of *security* [italics in original], the foundation on which peace has always existed. He had concentrated on building structures and institutions to run a world in which goodwill and understanding would reign supreme.[10]

Stalin, virtually the sole architect of Soviet foreign policy, was quite happy to play along. "As long as the Alliance lasted, Stalin believed he could outsmart Western leaders and continue the redistribution of spheres of influence ..."[11] is the view of two recent Russian historians, working with newly declassified Soviet documents. As far back as 1944, George Kennan, then a diplomat with the American embassy in Moscow, tried to warn Washington policymakers about Soviet attitudes toward Roosevelt's concept of trying to organize for peace:

> Western conceptions of future collective security and international collaboration seem naïve and unreal to the Moscow eye. But if talking in unreal terms is the price of victory, why not? If the Western World needs Russian assurances of future collaboration as a condition of military support, why not? Once satisfied of the establishment of her power in Eastern and Central Europe, Russia would presumably not find too much difficulty in going through whatever motions are required for conformity with these strange western schemes for collaboration and preservation of peace. What dangers would such collaboration bring to a country already holding in its hands the tangible guarantees of its own security, while prestige would demand that Russia not be missing from any councils of world power.[12]

The Yalta Conference opened on February 4, 1945. The Americans arrived with the long-term goal of gaining final Soviet approval on the formation of a peace organization, a structure to ensure peace, the United Nations. The rapid progress of the Allied armies made it necessary to also discuss

European political and military problems. A major goal of the United States and Great Britain was to get a fixed date for the Soviet Union to declare war on Japan. This was easy to settle. Stalin agreed that the Soviets would move against Japan three months after the Germans surrendered. Stalin kept this promise, likely in return for territorial concessions in Asia.

Another problem was the future role of France. Great Britain wanted France to play a full role in postwar Germany; the Soviets believed that France had not played much of a part in the war and should not play much in the peace. Eventually, they agreed that France could have a zone of occupation in Germany—not a problem for Stalin because this would come from American and British zones. France would have membership in the Allied control council for Germany. French leader Charles DeGaulle, however, would not be invited to attend Big Three meetings.

Permanently dismembering Germany into smaller states was discussed. This suggestion had been raised in late 1943, at the Big Three meeting in Tehran. The Yalta participants decided to pass the issue to a lower-level meeting, and nothing ever came of the proposal. Stalin, for one, was still thinking about a united Germany becoming Communist and an ally of the Soviet Union.

The three leaders discussed German reparations, requiring the Germans to make some effort to pay the material cost of the damage World War II had done. Churchill pointed out that Germany was so damaged by the war that the Allies could not hope to extract anything approaching the economic value of what they had spent, or lost, defeating Germany. German reparations after World War I had been paid with the help of loans from the United States. The official State Department minutes of the meeting noted that "... there had been only two billion pounds extracted from Germany in the form of reparations by the Allies after the last war and that even this would not have been possible had not the United States given Germany credit."[13]

Roosevelt responded to this, in the words of the minutes, "that he remembered very vividly that the United States had lost a great deal of money. He said that we had lent over ten billion dollars to Germany and that this time we would not repeat our past mistakes."[14] Roosevelt seems not to have anticipated how strong the United States would emerge from the war and added that the United States could not afford to aid the Germans economically.

Winston Churchill was strongest in raising the issue of the dangers of a starving Germany if too many reparations were demanded and taken. He focused on the fact that the Germans must be left enough resources to pay reparations. A starving Germany would benefit no one. Churchill was thinking of the way reparations were handled after World War I. Even though Germany paid reparations with loans from the United States, Germany was economically devastated. Poor economic conditions bred resentment, and laid the groundwork for Hitler. Realism at Yalta put limits on reparations.

A few years later, this same realism would intersect with the realities of dealing with the Soviet Union and evolve into the American and British desire to have the western portion of Germany get back on its feet economically. Economic viability in western Germany would enable the Germans to feed themselves and substantially cut the cost of occupation. Becoming part of the Western European economic system would also lock at least part of Germany into a democratic path. Control of Germany would be accomplished by tying West Germany to the Western European democracies both economically and militarily.

Even if Churchill and some members of the British and American staffs were thinking this far ahead, though, and they might well have been, these would not be good arguments to use with Stalin. Churchill was well advised to use the arguments he used, that Germany needed to keep enough resources to avoid destroying its economy and to be able to produce enough to pay what reparations were demanded. The leaders decided to leave the details to a commission. Reparations did not prove to be a major practical issue.

Soviet Foreign Minister Vyacheslav Molotov later complained, "We collected reparations after the war, but they amounted to a pittance."[15] The Soviets, however, took enough from their occupation zone in Germany to make it harder when they tried to create the German Democratic Republic, East Germany. Molotov, contradicting his earlier statement, commented on this dilemma. "Quietly, bit by bit, we had been creating the GDR, our own Germany. What would those people think of us if we had taken everything from their country? After all, we were taking from the Germans who wanted to work with us."[16]

The most controversial decision to emerge from Yalta dealt with the postwar Polish government. Poland had been divided between Germany and the Soviet Union in 1939 and was invaded by both that September. The Soviets were accurate when they told Churchill that the Nazi-Soviet pact of that year was made obsolete by the German invasion of the Soviet Union. By August 1944, the Soviet army had pushed the Germans back almost to Warsaw. On August 1, 1944, the Polish Home Army, the chief non-Communist resistance force, heard the sounds of German-Soviet combat not far to the east. They began an uprising against the Nazis, partly out of a desire to liberate themselves before the Soviets arrived. Stalin stopped his army in the area for several weeks as the Germans defeated the uprising, wiped out the Home Army, and almost obliterated Warsaw.

Just before leaving for Yalta, Churchill told his private secretary, "Make no mistake, all the Balkans, except Greece, are going to be Bolshevised, and there is nothing I can do to prevent it.

There is nothing I can do for Poland either."[17] Churchill was a realist, still steeped in the balance-of-power idea that had been the basis for British foreign policy for 300 years. In October 1944, for example, Churchill and Stalin had come to the "percentages" agreement on how much influence each nation would have in the Balkans. The Big Three eventually agreed that, until elections would be held, the Soviet-supported government of Poland would be the government, but with added non-Communist members.

The Polish borders have long been among the most arbitrary in the world. A look at maps of the area throughout the past 400 years reveals that Poland almost seems to move back and forth. With few natural borders in the central European plain, Poland could be anywhere people wanted it to be. Before World War II, Poland was a basically landlocked country between the main body of Germany and East Prussia. A small corridor gave Poland an outlet to the Balkan Sea. Recreated in 1945, Poland moved west, giving up territory to the Soviet Union in the east in exchange for German territory in the west.

At Yalta, Churchill and Roosevelt were dealing with a man, Stalin, more complex than he is normally given credit for, combining a sense of balance of power, Communist ideology, a fair amount of personal paranoia, and the overwhelming desire not to allow any further invasion of Soviet territory. Stalin had no compunction about taking the actions he thought particular circumstances demanded. In the past, he had shown himself willing to use extreme brutality, but this was not the only available method he had. "By 1945 one could find some rudiments of the revolutionary imperial paradigm in Stalin's foreign policy, but he was fully prepared to shelve ideology, at least for a time, and adhere only to the concept of a balance of power."[18]

The Yalta Conference would issue a statement grandly declaring that all countries had the right to choose their own form of government. Stalin made it clear what was his first priority. In discussing Poland's postwar future, the minutes of a Yalta meeting describe Stalin at one point saying,

> Mr. Churchill had said that for Great Britain the Polish question was one of honor and that he understood, but for the Russians it was a question both of honor and security. Throughout history, Poland had been the corridor for attack on Russia... It was not only a question of honor for Russia, but one of life and death.[19]

Roosevelt remained the most idealistic of the three leaders at Yalta. He maintained the desire for a postwar world based on mutual cooperation, not on power and spheres of influence. The last time he spoke to the American Congress, on March 1, 1945, Roosevelt summarized what he thought he had achieved at Yalta by stating that "The Crimea Conference ought to spell the end of the system of unilateral action, the exclusive alliances, the spheres of influence, the balances of power and all the expedients that have been tried for centuries—and have always failed."[20]

The main criticism of Yalta was that the United States and Great Britain surrendered Eastern Europe to the Soviet Union. Political commentators and historians also have complained that the Soviets broke their word—at least somewhat contradicting the first argument. The Soviet Army, however, already had control of most of Eastern Europe or would have this control before the war ended. Stalin had told one of his aides that the armies would impose the political systems where they stopped. This is what would happen. The arbitrary border that divided Europe evolved, one can say, simply because it could evolve. Each side imposed its system where its armies ended up.

Churchill and Roosevelt still needed Soviet cooperation, at least until the war with Japan was successfully completed. In accepting the borders, so to speak, of the Soviet area of influence, Churchill and Roosevelt were accepting reality. Whatever effect arbitrary borders may have on the people directly involved, they do have a certain logic for their creators.

Two years later, James F. Byrnes, who became American secretary of state two months after Yalta, wrote about the conference that "There is no doubt that the tide of Anglo-Soviet-American friendship had reached a new high. But President Roosevelt had barely returned to American soil when the tide began to ebb."[21]

2

The Soviet Perspective

Amajor event in the creation of the arbitrary border in
Europe occurred on April 12, 1945. U.S. President Franklin
Delano Roosevelt died. He was succeeded as president by Vice
President Harry S. Truman, formerly senator from Missouri.
Truman had very little foreign policy experience when he took
over as president. In a day when presidents customarily gave vice
presidents very little to do, Truman had met with Roosevelt only
a few times. Truman had not been kept informed of detailed
military and foreign policy issues. The atomic bomb, for example, came as a total shock to Truman.

Truman was not necessarily tougher than Roosevelt, but he
was less idealistic. Where Roosevelt might be inclined to compromise, Truman was more confrontational. James Byrnes, who
had attended Yalta with Roosevelt, became secretary of state on
July 3, 1945, four days before Truman and Byrnes left for the
final Big Three meeting at Potsdam. Byrnes had been Truman's
rival in 1944 for the Democratic vice presidential nomination.

On May 8, 1945, another major event had taken place.
Germany surrendered.

THEORIES OF SOVIET BEHAVIOR

Truman faced several military and foreign policy issues at the
last Big Three meeting, starting July 17, 1945, in the Berlin sub-
urb of Potsdam. He came into the continuing debate first on
how to explain Soviet behavior and then how to deal with this
behavior. This debate continues today, with Russian historians
now able to participate freely.

Several theories have emerged to explain Soviet behavior.
Some blame defensiveness, to the point of paranoia. Russia
always had a fair degree of defensiveness regarding the outside
world, bordering on xenophobia, the fear and hatred of those
who are different. The Soviet Union was, at least in this respect,
very much the successor state to imperial Russia. The Soviet
experience in World War II, with unbelievably high casualties
and damage, only contributed to this fear of foreigners.
Appreciating the damage Germany did and might do again was

After the death of Franklin D. Roosevelt on April 12, 1945, Harry S. Truman was sworn is as the thirty-third president of the United States. Truman had been vice president for only 3 months when Roosevelt's death catapulted him into the presidency.

not Soviet paranoia; it was realism. Some Soviet defensiveness about the United States was not a fear of the American military but of what they called American economic imperialism. They would not be the first ones to make this complaint.

A second theory of Soviet behavior blames it on sheer imperial aggressiveness, the Soviets taking over similar tendencies from tsarist Russia, with the addition of Marxist ideology. Inevitable world revolution might require some assistance—though the amount was a continuing subject of debate among the Soviet leadership. A third theory has the Soviets as ruthlessly opportunistic. Once the security of what was later called the "outer empire" was secured, once Eastern Europe was under Soviet control, the Soviets might probe for Western weakness but would make major moves only when they detected an opening. All three could explain Soviet behavior, and all could operate to some extent. The question would always be what Soviet efforts at easing relations represented, reality or tricks, and how to respond.

Currently, even with the increasing release of Soviet documents by the Russians, a single "unified theory" of Soviet behavior has not been created. When Truman took office, American policymakers could not look back on a successful Cold War. They could not know the Soviet perspective. American policymakers had to react based on what they knew at the time, but, as discussed later, some made very good guesses.

The idea of a preemptive effort to destroy the Soviet military capacity was rejected, to the extent that it was ever realistically considered. Though the Soviet Union, at its height, had a population only about 20 percent larger than that of the United States, it had a clear advantage in size of conventional forces immediately available. The United States was the only power with nuclear weapons until 1949 but had perhaps only 200 warheads. By the time American stockpiles reached anything resembling the massive levels of the later Cold War period, the Soviets had developed their own nuclear weapons.

Western leaders soon realized that all theories of Soviet behavior called for similar responses: stop specific Soviet efforts at expansion and remove the military weakness and economic instability that could provide the opportunity, or at least the temptation, for expansion efforts. Basically, the West had to create a boundary beyond which the Soviets would not be allowed to go. "Containment" of the Soviet Union became the method and the goal. The arbitrary border, soon called the Iron Curtain, became not just the limit of democracy but a defensive line. As noted in Chapter 1, arbitrary borders, at least from the point of view of their creators, tend to have some logic behind them.

Stalin's record did not encourage Western trust. The U. S. and British governments could not always tell whether a move was a response to something the Western Allies did, intentionally or not, signs of a "Communist offensive," or a sheer mistake. Some American policymakers even joked about these mistakes. Dean Acheson, who served in American foreign policy positions including secretary of state, later wrote to Harry Truman, "We used to say that in a tight pinch we could generally rely on some fool play of the Russians to pull us through."[22]

The Soviets had the reverse problem. Their command society, with all decisions from the top, would make them less likely to consider American and British mistakes as just that, mistakes. They had to be signs of a capitalist plot to encircle and destroy the Soviets. After all, back in 1919 and 1920, both countries had sent troops to support the anti-Communist "white" side in the Russian Civil War. The United States and Great Britain actually had tried to destroy the Soviet Union.

Truman faced all these considerations at Potsdam. He also faced a new factor. July 16, the day before the Potsdam Conference began, Truman received word of the successful test of the first atomic bomb. On July 24, Truman "casually mentioned to Stalin that we had a new weapon of unusually destructive force."[23] Truman was surprised that Stalin took the news so calmly. Thanks to the extensive penetration of the Manhattan Project—the project established to create the atomic bomb—by Soviet agents, Stalin already knew.

THREATS TO THE WEST

From the moment it took power in the October 1917 Russian Revolution, the Communist government was seen as a threat to Western democracies. This feeling never really went away, only being temporarily pushed to the background in 1939 when the Nazi Germans became a more immediate threat.

From a democratic point of view, there were similarities between the two systems. A recent history of Europe compares the two:

> ... the desire for total control by the leaders ... gave their regimes the similar appearance of dictatorships relying more on the will of one man than any governmental system. Their common use of extensive propaganda, police terror, one-party domination, efforts towards centralization and state

On July 16, 1945, Truman, the Soviet leader Stalin, and Prime Minister Churchill and his successor as prime minister after Churchill was defeated in 1945, Clement Atlee, met near Potsdam, Germany to discuss postwar arrangements in Europe.

planning, and conflicting and competing overlays of commit-tee structure further strengthened the appearance of similar-ity. [There were important differences in function and ideology, particularly towards the private sector economy.] Whatever the differences and similarities, these ... regimes were equally distant from traditionally democratic, parlia-mentary forms of government and saw no need of preserving or respecting them. Their presence rent the body politic of Europe.[24]

Joseph Stalin had become securely entrenched as leader of the Soviet Union in 1929, after having ruthlessly eliminated his competition. Stalin, to the degree he had an ideology other than power, supported one of the two main views of how Communism in the Soviet Union should respond to the rest of the world: "socialism in one country." This gave "priority to the cautious pursuit of economic recovery within Russia.... Ranged against this approach was the more radical Permanent Revolution favored by Trotsky. This incorporated proposals for revolution abroad and radicalism at home ..."[25] Leon Trotsky and his supporters considered the first Communist country, the Soviet Union, to have a moral responsibility to actively spread Communism throughout the rest of the world. The Soviet Union, by this theory, was thought to be safer in a Communist world, particularly a world it could dominate.

Trotsky was Stalin's main enemy in his quest for power. (Stalin first had Trotsky exiled, and then murdered.) Stalin always focused more on gathering and using power than on ideology. To the extent he cared about ideology, however, Stalin's opposition to Trotsky inclined him to take a different view of the ideology of the spread of Communism.

Stalin's basic paranoia, the feeling that those around him were out to get him, also leaked into his foreign policy ideology. He wanted to protect the national safety as well as his own safety. Marxism justified this, Stalin thought. In 1924, he declared, "Soviet power in Russia is the base, the bulwark, the refuge of the revolutionary movement of the entire world."[26] The Soviet Union had to be kept safe to serve as this base. Stalin, like the West after World War II, wanted to create an arbitrary border as a defensive line. At least before the war, with some exceptions this arbitrary border was the real border of the Soviet Union.

Stalin had a perceptive view of the weakness of the Soviet Union when he took power. He wanted to concentrate on building up national power before he thought of spreading revolution. Stalin thought the capitalists in Great Britain and France could not be trusted, perhaps an outgrowth of his own habit of turning on his friends when they were no longer needed. Paranoia, theory, and realism combined in Stalin's foreign policy. Realism let Stalin change tactics, for domestic political reasons as well as policy reasons.

In 1933, the Soviet Union and the United States established diplomatic relations. In 1934, the Soviets joined the League of Nations. In March 1936, Nazi Germany sent troops into the Rhineland section of western Germany, which had been demilitarized by the Treaty of Versailles. German troops had been ordered to retreat quickly if France showed signs of any military reaction. None came. Four months later, the Spanish civil war started. Fascist military forces under General Francisco Franco began their revolt to try to overthrow the Spanish republican government.

Germany and Italy began aiding Franco's forces. Germany used Spain as a testing ground for the reestablished German air force, the *Luftwaffe*. The Soviets supplied aid to the republican governmental forces, both to resist Germany and as a possible opportunity for the Communists to take power. Stalin cut off Soviet aid to the Spanish republicans about a year later. He saw he was backing a lost cause. Stalin also was making an effort to improve relations with Germany, including a nonaggression pact. Stalin did not want to risk hurting these efforts.

Germany annexed Austria in March 1938, in what became known as the *Anschluss*. Despite this being a specific violation of the Treaty of Versailles ending World War I, Great Britain and France did nothing. In September of that year, Hitler turned on Czechoslovakia. He wanted to annex the Sudetenland, the section of western Czechoslovakia jutting into German territory. Hitler's excuse was the Sudeten Germans, the dominant population of this area, and their desire for self-determination. British Prime Minister Neville Chamberlain and his French counterpart held two meetings with Hitler and Italian dictator Benito Mussolini in late September in Munich. The Czech president was kept waiting outside during the second meeting and was finally informed he would have to turn over about a third of his country or fight Hitler alone.

The Czechs asked Stalin for help because Stalin had been calling for an alliance against Germany. Stalin gave as the reason for not coming to Czechoslovakia's aid that the Soviets were denied permission to send troops through Poland or Romania. Stalin was prepared to support Czechoslovakia verbally, but not to risk war with Germany. In March 1939, Hitler took over the rest of Czechoslovakia. This at least seemed to bring to an end French and British passivity. There was little they could do for Czechoslovakia, but they did guarantee Polish security if Poland was attacked by Germany and if Polish national forces resisted.

Stalin began to negotiate openly with the British and French on how to handle Germany. He was also negotiating secretly with Hitler. Motivations for Stalin's foreign policy in this period are still debated, particularly with Russia only gradually declassifying and releasing Soviet-era documents. One train of thought is that Stalin looked to make some sort of arrangement with Hitler, to buy time if not long-term peace, because he was getting nowhere with Great Britain and France. A second view is that Stalin always intended to make some sort of agreement with Hitler. An extreme view is that Stalin thought a Soviet agreement with Hitler would lead to the Germans getting into a war with Great Britain and France. He may also have seen a war among the Western powers and Germany as not only good for Soviet security, in diverting all possible enemies, but an ideological opportunity. A modern historian writes that "... a Soviet leader close to Stalin told Czechoslovak communists that only a European war could pave the way to communist power in Germany and other European countries."[27]

Whatever the motivation, on August 22, 1939, Germany and the Soviet Union signed a trade deal. Two days later, in Moscow, they signed a nonaggression pact. A secret section of the treaty divided the territory between them, with the Soviets taking half of Poland as well as control over the Baltic states of Estonia, Latvia, and most of Lithuania. The U.S. government received an unconfirmed "leak" of the general contents of the treaty but did not publicize its contents.

World War II began on September 1, 1939, when Germany invaded Poland. On September 17, 1939, with the battered Polish armies making an effort to regroup, Soviet forces entered Poland from the east. The final Polish forces surrendered on October 5, 1939. Aside from some minor French attacks in the

SECRET ADDITIONAL PROTOCOL
German-Soviet 1939 Nonagression Pact

On the occasion of the signature of the Nonaggression Pact between the German Reich and the [Soviet Union] the undersigned plenipotentiaries of each of the two parties discussed in strictly confidential conversations the question of the boundary of their respective spheres of influence in Eastern Europe. These conversations led to the following conclusions:

1. In the event of a territorial and political rearrangement in the areas belonging to the Baltic States (Finland, Estonia, Latvia, Lithuania), the northern boundary of Lithuania shall represent the boundary of the spheres of influence of Germany and the U.S.S.R. In this connection the interest of Lithuania in the Vilna area is recognized by each party.

2. In the event of a territorial and political rearrangement of the areas belonging to the Polish state the spheres of influence of Germany and the U.S.S.R. shall be bounded approximately by the line of the rivers Narew, Vistula, and San.

The question of whether the interests of both parties make desirable the maintenance of an independent Polish state and how such a state should be bounded can only be definitely determined in the course of further political developments.

In any event both Governments will resolve this question by means of a friendly agreement.

3. With regard to Southeastern Europe attention is called by the Soviet side to its interest in Bessarabia. The German side declared its complete political disinterestedness in these areas.

4. This protocol shall be treated by both parties as strictly confidential.

Moscow, August 23, 1939.

For the Government of the German Reich v. Ribbentrop	Plenipotentiary of the Government of the U.S.S.R. v. Molotov

Ardennes area, the British and French provided no practical assistance to Poland.

Starting in May 1940, Hitler had a busy year. He conquered Western Europe, including France, throwing the British off the continent. German forces nearly conquered North Africa and in June 1941 still had a chance of doing so. Hitler also bailed out the Italians by taking over Greece and Yugoslavia. Stalin spent the year carrying out all the clauses of the trade agreement with Germany. Stalin also began to expand the artificial Soviet security border. He took over the Baltic states—Lithuania, Latvia, and Estonia—to increase the defensive buffer between Germany and the Soviet heartland. These states had been created after World War I in an effort to develop logical borders for national homelands. The Soviets also attacked, and nearly lost a war with, Finland.

On June 22, 1941, "Barbarossa: The Turn of Russia,"[28] began. Some 3 million German soldiers, along with thousands of tanks and airplanes, attacked along a thousand-mile front. The Soviets were caught napping. Stalin, anxious to keep the peace with Germany as long as possible, had ignored warnings, increasingly specific, about a pending German attack. British intelligence learned of the coming attack, and Winston Churchill personally passed on the warning. The Americans, too, passed on a warning. Both were ignored, with Stalin still suspicious of Western motives. Soviet intelligence in Japan, under Richard Sorge, also delivered a specific warning, which, like the others, was ignored.

By September, German columns were already 200 miles from Moscow. Hundreds of thousands of Soviet troops had been killed or captured. As Winston Churchill later wrote:

> Terrific blows had been struck by the German armies. But there was another side to the tale. Despite their fearful losses Russian resistance remained tough and unbending. Their soldiers fought to the death, and their armies gained in experience and skill. Partisans rose up behind the German fronts and harassed the communications in merciless warfare.[29]

The Germans had thought they might be welcomed as liberators, particularly in the areas to the west of Russia proper. This might have happened, but for the German behavior. Jews and Gypsies were not the only targets of murderous German behavior. Hitler had briefed his generals to wage a war of extermination, with no concern for the rules of "civilized" warfare. His words, as recorded by his senior general, were that "The war against Russia will be such that it cannot be conducted in a knightly fashion. This struggle is one of ideologies and racial differences and will have to be conducted with unprecedented, unmerciful and unrelenting harshness."[30]

The Soviets, particularly the leadership, brought into World War II a basic mistrust of foreigners. Even before Hitler, virtually every great European dictator, with the exception of Louis XIV of France, had invaded Russia. Hitler's invasion was especially brutal. An estimated 17 million to 31 million Soviets died in World War II, roughly half civilian, half military.[31] The combat took on a "no-quarter" aspect, with both sides fighting to the death. A sizable percentage of the Soviet military dead, however, died as prisoners of war of the Germans, starved, tortured or worked to death. The record of what the Soviets had suffered during the war made it likely that their first intent would be to safeguard their territory. Their desire to secure their homeland, starting with the arbitrary border that came to be called the Iron Curtain, had a foundation in experience. This was a fact with which the Americans and British would have to deal.

By the time of the final two Big Three meetings, Yalta and Potsdam, the British were convinced that the Soviets had inherited tsarist Russian expansionism. They also noticed that Stalin seemed to be trying to engage in some frank horse-trading of areas of influence, at least by implication. In October 1944, during a visit to Moscow, Winston Churchill handed Stalin a piece of paper on which he had divided Romania, Greece, Yugoslavia, Hungary, and Bulgaria by percentages of Soviet and British-American influence. Churchill later claimed the percentages were to apply only to wartime conditions and were designed to avoid clashes among the Big Three. Greece, however, was the only one of the five for which Churchill claimed Western predominance. It was also the only one of the five that did not go Communist. Yugoslavia, where influence was evenly split, went Communist but soon became effectively independent of the Soviet Union.

Big power security needs would take precedence over the needs and wishes of the local people. The presence of armies would arbitrarily decide the postwar local political system and the borders that marked the limits of these systems.

The Soviets were not only happy not to interfere, at least not immediately, with what the United States and Great Britain did in Western Europe, outside of Germany, but also wanted the Western allies not to interfere in Eastern Europe. Soviet Foreign Minister Vyacheslav Molotov wrote on the margins of a document on Poland, "Poland—a big deal! But how governments are being organized in Belgium, France, Greece, etc., we do not know.... We have not interfered because it is the Anglo-American zone of military action."[32]

SOVIET DOMESTIC POLICY

Domestically, Soviet efforts to defeat the Germans were aided by the combination of easing repression and appealing to Russian nationalism. It would not be exaggerating to say that the major problem the Germans faced was that they could not find a way to attack the Soviet Union without attacking Russia at the same time. Even the name Stalin gave to their war, "The Great Patriotic War," reflected this approach. The government gave the impression that this looser approach would continue after the war ended and that more attention would be given to the production of consumer goods.

This was not to be. The same tightening of controls that occurred in Eastern Europe took place in the Soviet Union itself. Stalin's January 1946 speech, declaring that the Soviets would focus on defense and industrialization, was an open statement of his postwar domestic policies as well as what an American newspaper called a declaration of the Cold War.

The parts of this new policy visible to the Western world were such events as the 1948 Communist coup in Czechoslovakia, the direct efforts against the independent-minded leadership in Yugoslavia, and the purges throughout Eastern Europe in response to Yugoslavia's going its own way. The same year saw Soviet moves against Berlin, and, in a major side front to the Iron Curtain, the start of the final campaign leading to the Communist takeover in China.

POST-STALIN ERA

Stalin died in March 1953. His death touched off a period of Kremlin liberalization. There were periods when Kremlin leadership would swing the pendulum back to repression, but never to the extent as under Stalin. The Soviet leadership was consciously trying to avoid a return to Stalinism. Group leadership took over, with Nikita Khrushchev eventually becoming the single dominant leader. The new era was shown by what happened to those who tried to overthrow Khrushchev in a "palace coup" in 1957. They stayed alive, though they were exiled to minor positions. Foreign Minister Molotov, for example, became ambassador to Mongolia. Liberalization of Kremlin rule was relative, however. Moscow still wanted to be in control but would first try to persuade Eastern Europe to follow its instructions.

Several of what might be called Kremlin eras followed Stalin. Group leadership characterized the period 1953 to 1957, with Khrushchev rising to become the prime leader. The Khrushchev era continued to 1964. This leadership was relatively liberal, with a few unfortunate exceptions such as Hungary in 1956. One such move was the Soviet pullback from Austria in 1955, after a treaty declaring Austria neutral. Austria was removed from the artificial border of the Iron Curtain because the Soviets no longer saw this as necessary. Placing it outside both sides' borders, so to speak, was seen as sufficient.

Initial peace feelers to the United States after Stalin's death, however, were rejected as Kremlin tricks. Such rejection may have been a lost opportunity, but after Stalin the Americans really had little reason to trust the Soviets. This was also a period of Soviet involvement in the "third world" and some dangerous adventurism in Cuba and Berlin, the latter following proposals to unify and neutralize Berlin itself or all of Germany.

Khrushchev was overthrown in 1964 by a group of plotters led by Leonid Brezhnev. The era of détente with the United States followed during the 1970s but ended with the Soviet invasion of Afghanistan in 1979, the only case of Soviet combat action outside Eastern Europe. Repression was the key at home, but what might be called "compassionate repression." Confinement in a mental hospital or internal exile were the methods of choice, not the firing squad.

The three years following Brezhnev's death in 1982 were marked basically by the advent to power of two Soviet leaders, Yuri Andropov and Konstantin Chernenko. Little happened because each died after less than two years in office. Andropov's main achievement was fostering the career of someone he promoted to the top ranks of Kremlin leadership, Mikhail Gorbachev.

Though opportunism and Russian expansionism played roles, probably the major Soviet motivation for the creation of the arbitrary border of the Iron Curtain was their perception, particularly Stalin's perception, of Soviet security needs. One interesting piece of evidence of this was a proposal Stalin made in March 1952, a year before he died, for four power talks to discuss the unification, rearmament, and neutralization of Germany. Stalin already saw the Communist regime in East Germany becoming as much a problem as an advantage to the Soviets. He also expected the imminent signing of treaties ending the occupation of West Germany and its incorporation, as an effectively independent state, in the European economic and defense communities. Stalin seemed willing to give up Communism in East Germany and to pull back the arbitrary border of the Iron

Curtain as a trade-off for avoiding a strong West Germany and for strengthening the Soviet defense and economic perimeter.

There is evidence that the proposal was a Soviet bluff; a way of testing the West's determination over West Germany, issued only with the near certainty nothing would come of the idea. Nothing did, and by the end of his life, Stalin had returned to a determination to make a Communist East Germany part of the Soviet system.

Interestingly, the far less hard-line Nikita Khrushchev became far more adventurous in trying to expand Soviet influence beyond the arbitrary border of the Iron Curtain. The Iron Curtain seemed to shift from the defensive limits of Soviet power to a base for further expansion. Within Eastern Europe, as will be discussed in the following chapters, Khrushchev's liberalization, ironically, led to the perceived need to use force more often and in greater scale than under Stalin. An old saying, the truth of which will become apparent in the last chapter, is that a repressive society is under the most danger when it tries to liberalize.

3

The American Perspective

Japan surrendered on April 15, 1945. The Soviets had kept their promise to declare war on Japan three months after the end of the war with Germany. Their forces were smashing through Japanese forces in Manchuria when the United States dropped atomic bombs on Hiroshima and Nagasaki.

In Eastern Europe, the Soviets were consolidating their control. The United States and Great Britain were growing surprisingly far apart as allies. The United States was seriously considering withdrawing from most of its involvement in Europe and started by suddenly canceling Lend-Lease, the primary program of aid for American allies during World War II.

The Soviets were cooperating in creating the United Nations. They also applied for a reconstruction loan from the United States. When they did not hear about the loan and inquired, they were told the papers had been lost during an agency move in Washington. This reason, perfectly believable to Americans and likely accurate, was not accepted in Moscow. It would not be the last culturally based misunderstanding between the two powers.

CHURCHILL'S "IRON CURTAIN" SPEECH

On February 9, 1946, the day before Supreme Soviet elections (with only one candidate for each seat), Joseph Stalin spoke on the need for Soviet rearmament. Stalin declared that rearmament would have to take priority over consumer needs. Stalin stressed the importance of unilaterally ensuring Soviet security. The Soviet Union must prepare to defend itself, Stalin said, against any threats. Stalin declared that "the unevenness of capitalist development usually leads in time to a violent disturbance of equilibrium,"[33] with war among capitalist camps.

The speech was interpreted in several ways. Later Russian historians noted that Stalin had already begun rearming the Soviet Union and developing an atomic bomb. Some Western historians have noted that Stalin seemed to be expecting war among the capitalists. Stalin was also aware that World War II had also started out as a war among the capitalists. American media, however, reported the speech as almost a declaration of cold

On February 6, 1946, Joseph Stalin spoke on the need for Soviet rearmament to ensure Soviet security. His speech provoked the two most influential statements of the western position at the start of the Cold War. These were George Kennan's "Long Telegram" of 1946 and Winston Churchill's "Iron Curtain" speech at Westminster College on March 5, 1946.

war. *Time* magazine reported the speech as "the most warlike pronouncement uttered by any top-rank statesman since V-J Day."[34]

Stalin's speech provoked possibly the two most influential statements of the Western position and policy at the start of the Cold War. George Kennan's "Long Telegram," sent February 22, 1946, before Churchill's speech, was inspired by an inquiry from Washington to the American embassy in Moscow asking for an explanation of why the Soviets seemed so reluctant to cooperate in the World Bank and the International Monetary Fund. Kennan's telegram, an 8,000-word report explaining a lot more than why the Soviets did not like multinational lending institutions, took several weeks to make its influence felt. (For full text of the "Long Telegram," see Appendix A.)

Winston Churchill responded publicly to Stalin on March 5, 1946. Churchill gave a speech at Westminster College, in Fulton, Missouri. President Harry Truman was on the platform when Churchill spoke. Churchill's speech was a "broad and sweeping overview"[35] of the state of the world just a few months after the end of World War II. Churchill aimed at doing in the United States regarding the Soviet Union what he had tried to do in the 1930s in Great Britain regarding Nazi Germany. He sought to motivate American public opinion to accept the challenge of responding to the Soviet Union.

Churchill had accepted the invitation to speak the November before, particularly since the written invitation had arrived with a handwritten note from Truman, expressing his hope that Churchill could make it and offering to introduce him. Churchill came to Florida in January 1946 to work on the speech. He met with Truman in early February to discuss what message he wanted to deliver. In early March, Churchill came to Washington to meet Truman. They would travel together on the presidential train to Missouri.

Secretary of State James Byrnes read a copy of the speech and gave Truman a summary of the contents. Truman initially decided not to read the speech itself, so as not to give Stalin the impression that Great Britain and the United States were ganging up on the Soviets. Copies had already been given out to the press on the train, and Truman probably soon realized that Stalin would not believe he had no idea of what Churchill was going to say. Truman read the speech.

The interesting thing about the speech is that its most memorable phrase, "From Stettin in the Baltic to Trieste in the Adriatic, an iron curtain has descended across the continent,"[36] was not the main focus of the speech. He was calling for the United States and Great Britain to act and react appropriately to the Iron Curtain. Churchill set the theme by declaring, in words applicable in 2004 as well as 1946, "The United States stands at this time at the pinnacle of world power... For with primacy in power is also joined an awe-inspiring accountability to the future."[37] (For full text of the speech, see Appendix B.)

Churchill spoke of the requirement for a guiding strategic concept to enable policymakers to focus on national and international needs. Most controversially in this country and in the

---

AN AMERICAN RESPONSE TO CHURCHILL'S IRON CURTAIN SPEECH

James Byrnes, Overseas Press Club, New York City, April 1946

Selections from Speech

"We have joined with our allies in the United Nations to put an end to war. We have covenanted not to use force except in defense of law as embodied in the purposes and principles of the Charter. We intend to live up to that covenant.

But as a great power and as a permanent member of the Security Council we have a responsibility to use our influence to see that other powers live up to their covenant. And that responsibility we intend to meet.

Unless the great powers are prepared to act in the defense of law, the United Nations cannot prevent war. We must make it clear in advance that we do intend to act to prevent aggression, making it clear at the same time that we will not use force for any other purpose ...

No power has a right to help itself to alleged enemy properties in liberated or ex-satellite countries before a reparation settlement has been agreed upon by the Allies. We have not and will not agree to any one power deciding for itself what it will take from these countries.

We must not conduct a war of nerves to achieve strategic ends.

We do not want to stumble and stagger into situations where no power intends war but no power will be able to avert war...."

Source: James F. Byrnes, *Address by the Honorable James F. Byrnes, Secretary of State, at the Overseas Press Club, New York City*, 1946. Washington, D.C.: U.S. Government Printing Office, 1946.

Soviet Union, he effectively called for an alliance between the United States and Great Britain, a revival of the "special relationship" between these two countries. He pointed out that "time may be short. Do not let us take the course of allowing events to drift along until it is too late,"[38] referring to his warnings about Nazi Germany ten years earlier, which Great Britain and France had ignored, instead allowing events to drift along. Time had not run out, though.

> I repulse the idea that a new war is inevitable; still more that it is imminent. It is because I am sure that our fortunes are still in our own hands ... that I feel the duty to speak out now ... I do not believe that Soviet Russia desires war. What they desire is the fruits of war and the indefinite expansion of their power and doctrines.[39]

Truman, when he finally read the speech, told Churchill that his speech would cause a stir. It did. Truman, a few days later, claimed that he did not know what Churchill was going to say and that because this country had freedom of speech, Churchill could say whatever he wanted to say. Much of the American press was not so polite, condemning Churchill's implied call for a military alliance between the United States and Great Britain. The historical American dislike of "entangling alliances" had not yet ended. Americans were still attracted to the idea of withdrawing from so active a role in the world, though they did not want to go back to the full-scale isolationism of the years before World War I. This withdrawal is what Churchill wanted to avoid.

The Labour government in Great Britain did not object to what Churchill said. Prime Minister Clement Atlee and Secretary of State for Foreign Affairs Ernest Bevin had been trying to achieve the same cooperation with the United States. They, like Truman, saw the need to slowly coax American public opinion and were worried about its immediate effect. The Soviets were, as might have been predicted, displeased. Stalin responded to the interview by saying, "There is no doubt that the policy of Mr. Churchill is a set-up for war, a call for war against the Soviet Union."[40]

THE LONG TELEGRAM AND THE SOURCES OF SOVIET CONDUCT

Washington decision makers liked what Churchill said but were concerned that he might be too far ahead of American public opinion. When Churchill made his speech, more and more decision makers were getting the chance to read Kennan's telegram. Kennan began by stating that he considered Soviet propaganda, internal and external, to accurately reflect the way the Soviets saw the rest of the world. He added that their assumptions were not true, but that this did not matter because they acted on their beliefs. "Soviet leaders are driven by necessities of their own past and present positions to put forward a dogma which pictures the outside world as evil, hostile and menacing ... "[41] This was their justification for isolating the Soviet population from the outside world and for increasing internal police power and external military powers, the organs of state security. Kennan saw this as a variation of Russian nationalism, but one made more dangerous in its appeal of Marxist ideology to the rest of the world.

The Soviets, Kennan wrote, expected no permanent coexistence with the West, particularly with the West's strongest power, the United States. The Soviets would compete with the West by what Kennan called "official" and "unofficial" means. Official means would focus militarily by building up Soviet strength and dominating the countries bordering the Soviet Union. This focus explained the increasing control over Eastern Europe. It also explained Soviet pressure on Turkey for free passage through the Dardanelles, including bases in the area, and the continued presence of Soviet troops in northern Iran.

The Soviets would participate in international organizations whenever the Soviets thought they could extend their power or dilute another's. The Soviets were participating in the politically based United Nations, where they could check "dangers" from the United States, but not in the economically-based World

Bank and International Monetary Fund, where they lacked the resources to play a major influential role. Kennan also saw the Soviets seeking to increase their influence in developing areas of the world, while trying to decrease Western influence. Kennan predicted well here. When the Iron Curtain in Europe, also called the Central Front, settled into a stalemate, and nuclear weapons made any attempted change highly dangerous, the Soviets would focus more efforts in the so-called third world.

"Unofficial" Soviet policy would support subversion of opposition governments and institutions within Western nations. Appropriate organizations, such as labor unions, would be infiltrated. The Soviet goal would be to "undermine general political and strategic potential of the major Western powers, hamstring measures of national defense, increase social and industrial unrest, stimulate all forms of disunity, poor set against rich, black against white, young against old, newcomers against established residents, etc."[42]

GEORGE KENNAN RECONSIDERS CONTAINMENT

[In] 1985, at a symposium at the National Defense University, Washington, D.C., the "creator" of containment, George Kennan, reconsidered his theory and how it had come to be applied in the years since. Keep in mind that what follows was written before the Gorbachev *glasnost* and *perestroika*.

"What I was trying to say, in the 'x' article, was simply this: 'Don't make any more unnecessary concessions to these people. Make it clear to them that they are not going to be allowed to establish any dominant influence in Western Europe and in Japan if there is anything we can do to prevent it. When we have stabilized the situation in this way, then perhaps we will be able to talk with them about some sort of a general political and military disengagement in Europe and the Far East—not before.' This, to my mind, was what was meant by the thought of 'containing' communism in 1946."

Source: George F. Kennan, "Reflections on Containment," in *Containing the Soviet Union: A Critique of US Policy*, edited by Terry L. Deibel and John Lewis Gaddis. Washington, D.C.: Pergamon-Brassey's International Defense Publishers, 1987.

Kennan dealt with ways to handle the Soviets. He pointed out that the Soviets did not like to take unnecessary risks and did not work by set timetables, in both cases unlike Hitler. When they met resistance, they would withdraw. At about the same time Kennan was writing the telegram, Western resistance led to the Soviet withdrawal from Iran and dropping demands for bases in Turkey. The West would have to stand up to the Soviet Union but should try to do so in ways that did not put Soviet prestige on the line. The West would have to provide nations with a better alternative to the future than the Soviets could provide. The West would also have to provide political and economic security.

Kennan's Long Telegram was a statement of this view for government. The views were advanced to the public, and the concept of "containment" created, in a paper written at the end of 1946 and published the next year in *Foreign Affairs* magazine. Kennan would later state that he was speaking politically when he wrote that:

> ... it is clear that the main element of any United States policy toward the Soviet Union must be that of long-term, patient but firm and vigilant containment of Russian expansive tendencies. It is important to note, however, that such a policy has nothing to do with ... threats or blustering ... While the Kremlin is basically flexible to its reaction to political realities, it is by no means unamenable to considerations of prestige. Like almost any other government, it can be placed by tactless and threatening gestures in a position where it cannot afford to yield even though this might be dictated by its sense of realism ...
>
> [Balanced against the dangers the Soviet Union presents] are the facts that Russia, as opposed to the western world in general, is still by far the weaker party, that Soviet policy is highly flexible, and that Soviet society may well contain deficiencies that will eventually weaken its own total potential. This would of itself warrant the United States entering with reasonable confidence upon a policy of firm containment,

designed to confront the Russians with unalterable counter-
force at every point where they show signs of encroaching
upon the interests of a peaceful and stable world ...

It would be an exaggeration to say that American behavior
unassisted and alone could ... bring about the early fall of
Soviet power in Russia. But the United States has it in its
power to increase enormously the strains under which the
Soviet policy must operate, to force upon the Kremlin a far
greater degree of moderation and circumspection than it has
had to observe in recent years, and in this way to promote
tendencies which must eventually find their outlet in either
the breakup or the gradual mellowing of Soviet Power."[43]

Kennan did not use the term "arbitrary borders" and probably
would not have liked the concept. The better term for what he
introduced might be "maximum borders," a limit to the expansion of influence but with the express purpose not just of
decreasing the area of Soviet influence but of changing or ending their government.

A response to Kennan's article, by influential political com-
mentator Walter Lippmann, appeared not long after. This article
first used the term "cold war." Lippmann agreed with much of
what Kennan said but differed on one key point. Kennan wanted
to contain the Soviets where they were. Lippmann, however,
thought Kennan was too pessimistic in seeing no possible settlement with the Soviets. Lippmann, agreeing with Stalin that the
arbitrary border was defined by the reach of armies, wanted to
move the Soviet army back into the Soviet Union. Lippmann
wrote that:

A genuine policy would ... have as its paramount objective a
settlement which brought about the evacuation of Europe.
This is the settlement which [sic] will settle the issue which
has arisen out of the war. The communists will continue to
be communists. The Russians will continue to be Russians.
But if the Red Army is in Russia, and not on the Elbe, the
power of the Russian communists and the power of the

Russian imperialists to realize their ambitions will have been
reduced decisively.[44]

Until then, Lippmann continued, "American power must be
available, not to 'contain' the Russians at scattered points, but to
hold the whole Russian military machine in check, and to exert a
mounting pressure in support of a diplomatic policy which has as
its concrete objective a settlement that means withdrawal."[45] This
sounds reasonable when responding to the theories that the
Soviets were pursuing imperial Russian expansionism or were
being ruthlessly opportunistic. Lippmann's ideas would likely have
little effect on the Communist ideological causes of Soviet behavior. Active pressure, real or apparent, on the Soviets, however,
would risk increasing paranoia to the degree that the Soviets might
perceive dangerous threats to their arbitrary defensive borders.

EARLY EXAMPLES OF CONTAINMENT

Kennan's Long Telegram and his article, with an occasional
foray on the peripheries into the more active Lippmann
approach, laid out what eventually proved to be the successful
American strategy for winning the Cold War. Had anyone at the
time written an article called "The Sources of American
Conduct," however, the article would have pointed out a pendulum effect in American policy creation, a swinging back and
forth between extremes. American policy varied from confrontational, sometimes ignoring or scoffing at possible Soviet
peace moves, to extremely cooperative, crediting the Soviets
with better intentions than they were showing. Kennan's position gave the desirable middle ground. Kennan had warned
against disunity, as well as placing too much emphasis on Soviet
behavior as responsive rather than working toward their own
objectives, and these policy switches probably confused as well
as contained the Soviets. These switches, though, were an
inevitable part of democratic government.

Kennan later said that he expected most Soviet threats to be
political and that responses should be political. In 1996, Kennan

stated in an interview in *U.S. News and World Report* that "I should have explained that I didn't suspect them of any desire to launch an attack on us."[46] Indeed, during the same period in which Kennan was writing his article, two cases occurred in which nonmilitary responses to the Soviets worked.

The winter of 1946–1947 was one of the coldest winters ever in Europe. Making things worse, European harvests in 1946 had been poor. During the winter, in Great Britain, better off than most of Europe, more stringent food rationing was put into effect than during World War II itself. Electricity was rationed. The total effect was to damage the British economy, pretty much halting its postwar recovery. The Labour government saw that cutbacks were necessary, starting with foreign commitments.

The most notable retrenchments were the colonial regimes in India and in Palestine, and aid to Greece. Partitioning of India and Pakistan, as well as Israel and Jordan, continues to make news today. At that time, Greece, still in the midst of a civil war between Communists and non-Communists, was considered the more urgent problem. On Friday afternoon, February 21, 1947, Great Britain informed the United States that its aid to the non-Communist Greek government would end in six weeks.

Not having realized the poor state of the British economy, American leaders were shocked. Under Secretary of State Dean Acheson had a busy weekend. By early the next week, Acheson's recommendations had been approved by Secretary of State George Marshall and President Truman. That Thursday, February 26, Truman met with the leaders of Congress to convince them. (The Republicans had taken control of both houses of Congress in the 1946 elections for the first time since 1930.) Acheson briefed the Congressional leaders, and gained their support.

On March 12, 1946, Truman announced his new policy in an address to a joint session of Congress. He called for $400 million in immediate aid to Greece and Turkey. He also requested the right to send American troops to administer the aid. More importantly, Truman announced what came to be known as the Truman Doctrine.

> The seeds of totalitarian regimes are nurtured by misery and want. They spread and grow in the evil soil of poverty and strife. They reach their full growth when the hope of a people for a better life has died. We must keep that hope alive. I believe that it must be the policy of the United States to support free peoples who are resisting attempted subjugation by armed minorities or outside pressures.[47]

The Marshall Plan was created a few months later. George Marshall, on a trip to Europe, saw first hand the poor economic conditions and the effects of the harsh winter. Marshall appreciated the need to revitalize Western European economies, particularly that of West Germany, as a counterweight to the Soviets. George Kennan, now back in Washington, was appointed to head the group designing the most appropriate plan to provide this aid.

Kennan's main proposal was that the Europeans themselves would decide what they needed and present a unified request to Washington. He insisted that the offer be made to all of Europe. If Eastern Europe did not join, and Kennan expected they would not join, this would be their decision. Stalin, as part of a crackdown on growing nationalism in Eastern Europe, forbade them from joining. In his June 5, 1947, speech at Harvard University announcing the plan, Marshall claimed, inaccurately but dramatically, that it was not directed against any country or doctrine "but against hunger, poverty, desperation and chaos. Its purpose should be the revival of a working economy in the world so as to permit the emergence of political and social conditions in which free institutions can exist ..."[48]

The Marshall Plan certainly strengthened the arbitrary border of the Iron Curtain. The plan increased the strength of the Western European economies, making them less vulnerable to the potential political appeal of Communism. By being better able to resist Soviet expansionism, they became less tempting as targets.

AMERICA POST MARSHALL PLAN

These were not quiet times in the world from the American perspective. America saw the Soviets institute a year-long ground blockade of Berlin, in an attempt to force the Western allies to withdraw. In 1949, the North Atlantic Treaty Organization (NATO) was established. In 1950, the United States led an effort to stop the North Korean invasion of South Korea it took three years to restore the situation (the arbitrary border at the 38th parallel) that existed before the war. In 1952, Harry Truman decided not to run for a second full term as president of the United States. The Republican candidate, Dwight D. Eisenhower, replaced him. Eisenhower took office in January 1953, two months before Joseph Stalin died.

After Eisenhower took office, the United States continued in what came to be called the "Joe McCarthy" era, after the junior senator from Wisconsin. McCarthy was noted as the most visible, but not the only, Congressional "red baiter," allegedly trying to root out Communist influence in government and other aspects of American life. Accusations became enough to ruin careers, though no one ever actually went to jail solely for being a Communist. McCarthy and his types missed the real Communist agents in places such as the State Department and discredited legitimate concern about Soviet activities. McCarthy eventually went too far and was censured by the Senate.

America also continued in a period of unprecedented economic growth and self-confidence. The self-confidence sputtered with the Soviet launching of *Sputnik* in 1957. This set off strong national concern about what was considered a growing and dangerous gap in technology, science education, and weapons.

Eisenhower brought extensive foreign affairs experience to the White House from his services during World War II and as NATO commander. He recognized the need for a strong defense to enable the United States to counter Soviet expansionism and to avoid giving the Soviets the opportunity to take advantage of Western weakness. Eisenhower was strongly anti-Communist and favored what became known as "roll-back," doing what one could to free "captive" nations from Soviet control. This policy was moderated from the activist views Eisenhower expressed during the presidential campaign.

The United States would negotiate with the Soviets, but it would also choose where and when to resist Soviet aggression. Specific measures taken under this policy included the American Central Intelligence Agency's helping restore the Shah of Iran to power in 1953 and overthrowing a leftist government in Guatemala in 1954. Eisenhower believed that the Cold War could be won but that this would happen as a result of internal economic strains in the Soviet bloc. Eisenhower was prepared to resist the Soviets militarily, but this was not his first choice. In 1956, he told a Republican senator "I want to wage the cold war in a militant, but reasonable, style whereby we appeal to the people of the world as a better group to hang with than the Communists."[49]

Eisenhower was a traditional Republican conservative when it came to spending. He recognized that extensive arms spending could also damage the American economy. Nuclear weapons became favored. "More bang for the buck" was the informal phrase designed to reflect that nuclear weapons were cheaper, relative to destructive power, than conventional weapons. "Massive retaliation" was the more ominous description of the basic American policy to prevent a Soviet attack in Europe by threatening to use nuclear weapons against the Soviet Union.

On May 7, 1954, French forces under siege in Vietnam, at Dien Bien Phu, surrendered to Communist-nationalist Viet Minh forces. Several months later, the leadership of the Viet Minh was persuaded by the Chinese to agree to the "temporary" partition of Vietnam at the 17th parallel and the withdrawal of all foreign troops.

This divided Vietnam into North and South Vietnam, with North Vietnam Communist. The French withdrew, to be replaced by gradually increasing American involvement. The United States had initially resisted direct involvement. Dulles wrote in a memo that the United States "could not afford to send its flag and its own military establishment and thus to engage the prestige of the United States"[50] unless it expected to win.

Eisenhower added an ideological reason to nonintervention, the United States's reputation as anticolonial. "The standing of the United States as the most powerful of the anti-colonial powers is an asset of incalculable value to the Free World ... The moral position of the United States was more to be guarded than the Tonkin Delta, indeed than all of Indochina."[51] The only consistency in drawing lines in Europe, Vietnam, and Korea seemed to be that they were intended as temporary measures reflecting real areas of outside control.

American policy toward the Soviet Union, like Soviet policy toward the United States, continued to swing back and forth around what might be called the ideal middle. John F. Kennedy was elected president in 1960. Kennedy was almost 30 years younger than Eisenhower and had run for office on a platform of more vigorous opposition to Communism. This included correcting a "missile gap" with the Soviets, which turned out not to exist. Kennedy's administration saw the two most dangerous confrontations with the Soviets: Berlin in 1961 and Cuba in 1962. It also saw a treaty banning atmospheric nuclear testing, the first such treaty between the superpowers.

After Kennedy's November 1963 assassination, he was replaced by Lyndon Johnson. The Johnson era became noted for striking changes at home, both the civil rights revolution and the social changes of the 1960s. Johnson's time in office also saw escalation of American involvement in South Vietnam from roughly 20,000 combat advisors to 500,000 combat troops. Massive protests against the war were sparked by heavy American casualties with no clear results. These protests did not stop the war. They did help drive Johnson to decline to seek reelection in 1968 and his replacement as president by Richard Nixon.

Nixon first escalated the Vietnam War and then eventually ended American combat involvement. He also ended the draft. The Nixon administration brought about the somewhat surprising era of détente, closer cooperation with the Soviet Union and China. Nixon, as a congressman and senator in the late 1940s and early 1950s, had been an active red baiter, though never going as far as McCarthy. The most interesting part of détente directly concerning the Iron Curtain were the Helsinki Agreements, signed in 1975 after two years of negotiations. These agreements called for respect for human rights within all the signatories. These agreements also formally stabilized the informal stability of the Central Front of the Cold War by declaring the current frontiers secure and unassailable—including the borders between East and West Germany.

The spirit of détente continued throughout most of the decade, after Nixon resigned from office to be replaced by Gerald Ford and then Jimmy Carter. The desire for cooperation with the Soviets came to a crashing halt with their 1979 invasion of Afghanistan.

Ronald Reagan defeated Jimmy Carter in 1980. By the time he took office in 1981, Reagan was less impressed than his predecessors with the arbitrary border splitting Europe for 35 years. Reagan's first years in office came to be called "The New Cold War."[52] He embarked on a program of extensive expansion of the American military, though it was actually started by Carter. Reagan began to refer to the Soviet Union as the "evil empire." Reagan is considered a conservative ideologue. Any thought he might have given to different policy, however, was made virtually impossible by Soviet political turmoil during the last one or two of the Brezhnev years and the terms of his two brief successors, Andropov and Chernenko.

Reagan did respond to the opportunities presented when Mikhail Gorbachev took office in 1985. Most dramatically, in a June 1987 visit to the Berlin Wall, he echoed John F. Kennedy when he said, "Mr. Gorbachev, open this gate. Mr. Gorbachev, tear down this wall." Less dramatically, but more interestingly, Reagan ended his brief speech with "This wall will fall. It cannot withstand faith. It cannot withstand truth. The wall cannot withstand freedom."[53]

4

1948—Berlin

The year 1948 was important in the life of the ultimate arbitrary border, the Iron Curtain, focusing on Berlin and on the growing move toward an Atlantic alliance. The background to the events of that year actually began in June 1947 as British Foreign Secretary Ernest Bevin listened to radio reports of George Marshall's Harvard speech. Several months later, Bevin described what he felt listening to the speech. "I remember with a little wireless set alongside the bed," he said, "just turning on the news and there came this report of the Harvard speech. I assure you ... that it was like a lifeline to a sinking man. It seemed to bring hope when there was none. The generosity of it was beyond my belief."[54]

Ernest Bevin, a former British labor union leader, had served as minister of labor in Winston Churchill's coalition cabinet in World War II. With Clement Atlee's victory in 1945, Bevin switched to foreign secretary. Bevin soon became a strong advocate of coordinated Western action not only to meet but also to discourage what he saw as a Soviet threat. A key element in this coordinated action was keeping the United States fully involved in the defense of Europe. In the previous months, Bevin had detected an American desire to withdraw from active involvement, though perhaps not a full return to pre-World War II isolation. Marshall's speech told Bevin the United States was not withdrawing.

The next morning, Bevin sent a message to the American State Department that the British were approaching the French to discuss an appropriate response. Two weeks later, Bevin flew to Paris to meet with his French counterpart. The main issue they faced was how to handle whether the Soviet Union should be invited to join the plan. They reached the politically necessary compromise that the Soviets would be invited to join. Foreign ministerial meetings in Paris at the end of June showed that the West would not have to worry about the Soviets disrupting the Marshall Plan from inside. The Soviets used the meetings for anti-American propaganda, accusing the United States of designing the plan as a method of "political and economic subjugation of Europe,"[55] as it was described in a secret memo to Stalin.

The Soviet response was not just refusing to join the Marshall Plan. They refused to let Eastern European nations take part. Stalin also decided to increase his control over these states by getting rid of all non-Communist elements from their governments and by locking them into an organization called Cominform, the Information Bureau of the Communist Parties. Headquarters would be set up in Belgrade. A building was actually under construction when Tito's independence got Yugoslavia thrown out of the Cominform. The intended headquarters became a tourist hotel.

Over the next several years, Stalin undertook a series of purges in Eastern Europe, resulting in the arrests and executions of many leading Communists. The West saw Stalin reverting to the same terror tactics he had used in the Soviet Union ten years earlier.

Stalin's actual reasoning for vetoing Eastern European and Soviet participation in the Marshall Plan may have had as much to do with his own desire to keep control of the situation in his new "outer empire," as it came to be called, as from any desire to solidify the effective arbitrary border between West and East. The net effect, however, was to do just that, to tie the Communist nations of Eastern Europe to the Soviet economy, to place another barrier in the way of contacts within Europe.

In mid-1948, as the American presidential campaign was getting started, the United States Congress passed legislation to put the plan into effect. By 1952, $13 billion in American economic aid, a huge amount in the dollars of the day, went to Western Europe.

POLITICAL DEVELOPMENTS

Even good deeds have consequences, and political results began to follow in Europe. In February 1948, the non-Communist members of the coalition government in Czechoslovakia resigned. The Czech president did not call for new elections but allowed the Communists to form their own government. The only non-Communist was Jan Masaryk, the foreign minister. Three weeks later, Masaryk's body was found below the fourth floor window of his apartment. Masaryk's death was announced as suicide and could have been. His death was very convenient for the Communists, however, and the murder theory was widely accepted, even within Czechoslovakia.

On May 15, 1948, though they likely did not know it at the time, a major side issue to the Iron Curtain arose. This issue continues today, over a decade after the fall of the Iron Curtain, arose. The Jewish population of Palestine declared their section of the territory, from the United Nations ordered partition of late 1947, to be the State of Israel, the first independent Jewish state in 2,000 years. Almost immediately, Israel's Arab neighbors invaded Israel. The United States was the first country to recognize the new country. The Soviet Union was the second. Stalin saw a potential ally in the socialist Israeli government. This warm feeling would not last as the Soviets realized Israel was also democratic and pro-Western. Arms supplied by Eastern Europe, however, played a major role in allowing Israel to win its 18-month war of independence.

On January 13, 1948, in the British House of Commons, Ernest Bevin called for "some form of union"[56] in Europe to stem further Soviet expansion. This union would be backed by the United States and the British dominions. Bevin was careful not to propose that the United States join a formal alliance with Europe. Bevin did, however, propose to the French that they join with the British in offering a defense treaty to Belgium, the Netherlands, and Luxembourg.

The American State Department guessed, accurately, that Bevin was interested in having the United States involved in an Atlantic alliance. Secretary of State Marshall's senior advisors took different views on the idea. George Kennan favored the Europeans forming such an alliance but did not think the United States should initially join. Kennan thought that the Soviets were not planning a military attack on the West and that therefore an American guarantee was sufficient.

John D. Hickerson, a senior official in the Office of European Affairs, was one of those who took the opposite view from Kennan. Hickerson thought that to be really effective, a military alliance would require active American participation from the start. Whatever the reality of the Soviet threat, the Europeans felt such a threat existed. Assuming that the Soviets' intentions were peaceful would be risky.

Events of the next several months seemed to show that the Soviets were anything but peaceful. The Czech coup was followed almost immediately by increasing Soviet pressure on Norway to sign a treaty of friendship. Norway was determined to resist and asked the British if they would offer military assistance.

On March 5, 1948, the American military commander in Germany, Lucius D. Clay, telegraphed the Chief of Staff of the Army, "For many months, based on logical analysis, I have felt and held that war was unlikely for at least ten years. Within the last few weeks, I have felt a subtle change in Soviet attitude which I cannot define but which now gives me a feeling that it may come with dramatic suddenness."[57]

One week later, the British were informed that the United States wanted to proceed to discussions on an Atlantic security system. The British responded that a delegation would arrive in Washington on March 22. Five days before, the British and French signed a defense treaty with Belgium, Luxembourg, and the Netherlands. British, Canadian, and American representatives met for what they thought were secret talks at the Pentagon. Unfortunately, a junior member of the British delegation was Donald Maclean, later exposed as a Soviet agent. Talks ended April 1. The same day, the Soviets briefly halted Western trains to Berlin.

CURRENCY REFORM IN GERMANY

The preliminary talks for what became the North Atlantic Treaty Organization may have affected Soviet timing, but they were neither the provocation for nor the cause of what happened next. The United States and Great Britain had decided that restoring the economy of the parts of Germany under their control was necessary for Western European security. They persuaded the reluctant French to go along with measures that led, on May 24, 1949, to what can be considered the "independence day" of the Federal Republic of Germany, better known during the Cold War as West Germany. The West German "Basic Law," meant as a temporary measure until German reunification, went into effect.

Stalin responded to these measures, themselves responses to the perceived Soviet threat, by seeking to further harden his control over the Soviet sector of Germany. This required getting the Western allies out of Berlin. In this way, Stalin would eliminate the oddity and "bad" example of freedom presented by this small area outside his control, but existing on his side of the arbitrary border. Stopping the trains was just a preliminary measure, and access was soon restored.

About the same time the preliminary NATO talks were under way, the United States, Great Britain, and France decided to introduce a common currency in their German occupation zones. Currency reform was seen as a major first step in the financial and economic rehabilitation of Germany. This reform was viewed as helping to economically rehabilitate Western Europe, already recognized as an interconnected area. Interestingly, the Western powers moved to put the new currency into effect when they discovered the Soviets were printing new currency in East Berlin printing plants. They feared that if the Soviets introduced the new currency in their zone, this would free up old currency for use in pro-Communist political activities in the West.

Currency reform in the Western occupation zones of Germany would have the practical effect of hardening the economic part of the arbitrary border between them and the Soviet zone. This hardening can be credited to Soviet fears as much as Western intent. Soviet fears of greater economic integration between the two parts of Germany, as well as loss of political control and what they saw as military security, led them to take measures to secure their control. These measures would lead to the creation, on October 7, 1949, of the German Democratic Republic, usually called East Germany. The Federal Republic of Germany had been established on May 24, 1949. Both sides, however, first had to get through the Berlin blockade.

Berlin was specifically excluded from the Western-sponsored currency reform. On June 22, 1948, the four-power council still directly controlling Berlin decided not to discuss currency reform in the city. The next day, the still unified Berlin city council defied Soviet threats and a hostile pro-Communist mob, to turn back Soviet efforts to defeat reform. The day after that, the Soviets cut off all land communications to West Berlin. Within a few days, all supplies to the city were cut off, including electricity.

General Lucius Clay, American commander in Germany, immediately proposed that an armored convoy effectively fight its way to Berlin. He first proposed this to the British commander in Germany, General Sir Brian Robertson, who immediately rejected the idea as too dangerous. Robertson had anticipated the Soviet move and already had been studying an alternative. British figures showed that it would be possible to fly food and supplies, particularly coal, into Berlin by air. Both governments quickly approved, and the first flights began on June 26.

Technical problems had to be worked out. Landing fields in Berlin were not equipped to receive coal. Some B-29 bombers had been sent to Great Britain as a kind of subtle threat to Stalin, but he likely knew they were not configured to carry nuclear weapons. One B-29 had its bomb bay loaded with coal. It flew low over the Berlin Olympic Stadium, remaining from the 1936 Olympics, and opened the doors. Unfortunately, when the coal hit the floor of the stadium it was pulverized into useless coal dust. In further "coal drops," the coal was wrapped in canvas bags, which made it possible to unload the coal normally.

With flights eventually landing in Berlin 24 hours a day, sometimes as little as a minute apart, and with the necessity to skimp on aircraft maintenance, sheer technical accidents were certain. The first crash occurred on July 9. Two weeks later, a C-47 coming into Berlin's main Tempelhof Airport, crashed into an apartment building. The two pilots were killed, and the building was damaged, but there were no casualties on the ground. Berliners put up a plaque at the crash site reading "You gave your lives for us"[58] and brought flowers every day.

In August of 1948, about two months after the airlift began, the American commander at Tempelhof received a letter from a writer who called himself a resident of the Russian sector:

> Yesterday afternoon I have been standing for a while on the Railroad Station, Tempelhof ... watching the coming and going of the ... airplanes. Everytime when one of the big planes appeared on the western horizon and started to land there was a light on the faces of the people. Probably you can't imagine what every single plane means to us people, who are strictly separated from the western sectors because of the will of our occupation forces ... [The writer suggested that the planes] fly a little further sometimes so that in our sector the people will know too: "The Western Powers don't let us down."[59]

The letter writer asked to remain anonymous, because "the Russian secret service is quick on hand if it means to let someone disappear forever."[60]

The writer might not have been pleased if he knew of the difficulties of the airlift. Major General William H. Tanner, deputy commander of the Military Air Transport Service, had taken command of the airlift in July 1948. One of his flights into Berlin was Friday, August 13, 1948, a rainy, nasty day in Berlin. Tunner discovered that one cargo plane had crashed; a second had run off the runway after bursting a tire while trying to avoid the first plane. A third, landing on a second runway under construction, ended up stuck in mud. Tunner identified himself to the air traffic controllers and ordered all planes, except his, sent back to West Germany. Henceforth all planes got one pass at landing. They would either land or head back west. The very limited airspace over West Berlin had virtually no room for circling.

During the Berlin blockade the Soviets cut off all land communications to West Berlin. The British and the American decided that it would be possible to fly food supplies into Berlin and the airlift began on June 26, 1948. These efforts continued for 11 months. Here, some children in West Berlin are perched on a fence nearby Tempelhof airport to watch the fleets of U.S. airplanes bringing in supplies to circumvent the Russian blockade.

Tunner was particularly embarrassed because of the reason he had come to Berlin. There was a ceremony designed to honor the efficiency of the airlift. Tunner later wrote that the dignitaries on the ground were waiting in the rain as the commander of the airlift "was flying around in circles over their heads. It was damned embarrassing. The commander of the Berlin Airlift couldn't get himself into Berlin."[61]

Less embarrassing was the custom established by one of Tunner's pilots, Lieutenant Gail Halversen. He hitched a ride to Berlin on one of his days off, just to get the chance to see the city. Normally, pilots waited by their planes during the few minutes they were on the ground. About 30 children soon gathered as he stood watching landings at Tempelhof. He gave out a few sticks of gum and then promised the children that he would drop candy from his plane the next day. Halversen prepared some small packages of candy with their own tiny parachutes and kept his promise. By the time Halversen went back to the United States in January 1949, his efforts had attracted national attention and the assistance of many other pilots. Some 250,000 candy parachutes had been dropped. Other American pilots took over and the effort continued to the end of the airlift.

The Berlin blockade was ended on May 4, 1949, and the airlift stopped soon afterward. On June 20, the four occupying powers formally agreed to ensure normal functioning of rail, water, and road transport between Berlin and West Germany. During the months of the airlift, 2.3 million tons of food, fuel, and medical supplies had been flown into the city.

The Soviets had underestimated the ability of the United States and Great Britain to undertake a successful airlift. The last time the Soviets had encountered such an airlift was at the 1942–1943 Battle of Stalingrad. The Germans had tried, unsuccessfully, to airlift supplies to the German army the Soviets had trapped in the city. Ironically, General Tunner had gotten a German veteran of the attempted airlift to help with the Berlin effort.

The Americans and British learned several lessons from the airlift. They learned restraint but also the need to demonstrate a commitment to the people of Berlin, of Germany, and of Western Europe. Technically, as the Soviets always noted, Berlin was behind the arbitrary border of the Iron Curtain. Berlin was an outpost of freedom, however, a symbol of Western commitment to democracy. The Iron Curtain was not just an arbitrary border between democracy and Communism but also a defensive line for democracy, a limit to the expansion of Soviet control in Europe. Maintaining this border required a practical as well as a verbal commitment.

As a result of the Berlin blockade and airlift, the United States and Great Britain learned the need to keep sufficient troops in Europe to meet a conceivable Soviet threat, in what would likely be a "come as you are" conflict—with little time to bring in reinforcements. Next time, without forces on the ground, the Western allies might not be so lucky in finding a course of action between retreat and nuclear war.

A 1961 American study of Berlin, written at the time of the next Berlin crisis, noted that:

> First, Berlin held out during the blockade by a very narrow margin. A small decline in the amount of coal being flown in, for example, could have produced a breakdown. Secondly, any dilatory action in commencing the airlift, or any indication of Western retreat, might easily have produced defeatism on the part of the Berliners at the outset of the blockade ...[62]

One important lesson from the crisis, though seen from the perspective of the historian, was the restraint shown on both sides. The Americans and British had rejected a direct ground attack on Soviet forces. The Soviets made sure never to intentionally shoot down any airlift airplanes, though there remained the chance of a dangerous accident, with unforeseen results. With some dramatic exceptions, this practice evolved into a system of "managing" the Cold War, in Europe and outside. Except for Berlin, for example, every major confrontation of the Cold War would occur, however dangerous it might become, in peripheral areas, such as Korea and Cuba. The status quo might be undesirable, but change might be suicidal.

Berlin itself next came into the news 12 years later.

5

1961—
Berlin Again

In June 1961, Walter Ulbricht, long-time Communist Party leader and effective boss of East Germany, denied his government had any intention of building a wall between East and West Berlin. Ulbricht stated, probably indignantly, "The construction workers of our capital are for the most part busy building apartment houses, and their working capacities are fully employed to that end. Nobody intends to put up a wall."[63]

On first glance, a wall would seem a strange solution to the East German problem, the near hemorrhaging of the "best and brightest" to freedom in the West. The wall would cut off the free flow of people between the two parts of the city, which helped the economy of both sides. In June, the Berlin Crisis of 1961, the second most dangerous moment of the Cold War, had not heated up. Putting up a wall would provide the West an excellent symbol of the oppressive nature of a system that needed a wall to keep its own people from leaving. A wall would provide the leader of the free world a chance to dramatically and memorably point this out. A wall, 28 years later, could also provide one of the greatest moments ever seen on television: a birth of freedom.

In 1961, a wall would be a symbol that the arbitrary border of the Iron Curtain was losing all logic aside from the arbitrary will of its creator.

THE NEW FRONTIER

The election of 1960 guaranteed a generational change in American leadership. President Eisenhower was 70. Vice President Richard Nixon, 48, or Senator John F. Kennedy, 43, would succeed him. The election turned out to be one of the closest the country had seen—in recent time, the closest up to the election of 2000. In an election as close as that of 1960, it becomes hard to see a clear mandate for change. Change, however, was the message Kennedy projected, the message that Eisenhower had not been tough enough with the Soviets. Kennedy would stand up to the Soviets, whether in Europe or in the growing competition in the developing world. He would also

On September 9, 1961, an East Berlin policeman puts a brick in place to heighten the wall to 15 feet, while residents in a neighboring building look on.

respond to any signs of Soviet desire to cooperate. As he said in his inaugural address, he would "never negotiate out of fear, but never fear to negotiate."[64]

Kennedy's inaugural message to the Soviets may have been a bit confusing, conveying elements of confrontation and of cooperation. Kennedy, however, was also responding to a tough-minded speech Nikita Khrushchev made on January 6, 1961, the time Kennedy would have been picking his cabinet and preparing his speech. Khrushchev had declared a continuing struggle with the West, but one to be carried out short of war. In June of that year, an expert on Soviet strategy tried to analyze the speech for a Senate committee. The expert stated:

> ... There is a new administration and [Khrushchev] feels compelled ... to show that he is not going to be intimidated ... that ... he is going to continue on his merry way ... He wants to test our resolution, as he has done in earlier instances. Above all, he wants to intimidate the new leaders ... An old Communist

trick is to execute "tests of strength" at the beginning of a new administration to find out how far they can go.[65]

By the time this was written, Kennedy had also given Khrushchev two examples of, if not his resolution, then his judgment. They would soon create major problems.

BAY OF PIGS AND VIENNA

According to his predecessor, Dwight D. Eisenhower, Kennedy faced three immediate foreign policy problems: Laos, Berlin, and Cuba. Laos was the first to arrive, so to speak, in March 1961. The situation in that country, with a Communist rebel movement, deteriorated enough to require the dispatch of some American troops to the Laos-Thailand border. By the time this was seen as insufficient to calm down the situation in Laos, it was already late April 1961. With the failure of the Bay of Pigs invasion of Cuba, Kennedy was far more inclined toward a negotiated settlement. The one success of Kennedy's July meeting with Nikita Khrushchev in Vienna, Austria, was agreement on a neutral Laos, with a formal agreement signed on July 23, 1962. This agreement lasted ten years, until the wars in Vietnam and Cambodia spilled over into Laos.

Cuba was next. Kennedy had inherited a Central Intelligence Agency (CIA) plan for an invasion of Cuba to overthrow Fidel Castro and his Soviet-supported Communist government. The ground forces for the invasion would be Cuban exiles, but they would have full American support, particularly air support. Kennedy rejected the CIA proposal, ordering minimal American involvement. He wanted to be able to deny any American involvement, not exactly a vote of confidence for the idea. Kennedy's changes pushed an already questionable plan into probable failure. Poor implementation, combined with Fidel Castro's quick and expert response, resulted in an embarrassing fiasco.

Kennedy learned to rely less on so-called experts in making foreign policy. This distrust would have valuable results in the Cuban Missile Crisis of October 1962. Kennedy rejected the

October 1962 military recommendation of immediate air strikes on Cuba to destroy Soviet missiles in Cuba, followed by an invasion. This move probably would have touched off a nuclear war with the Soviet Union. It remains uncertain how Kennedy would have reacted to military advice to send American combat troops to Vietnam.

Kennedy had wanted to send to the Soviets the message that the new American leadership was tough and determined, that it knew what it was doing and could not be pushed around. The message he actually sent at the Bay of Pigs was just the opposite, that he was a weak leader and his administration did not know what it was doing. The message was almost what is sometimes called "worst case," that of aggressive intent and weakness. This message was only reinforced by the Vienna summit meeting with Nikita Khrushchev, June 3–4, 1961.

To the bad image he took to Vienna, Kennedy added physical problems. His famous bad back, known at the time, was apparently in particularly bad shape. He was taking injections of procaine, a local anesthetic, for the back pain. Kennedy also suffered from Addison's disease, something not known at the time. Immediate symptoms of this disease would have been weakness and emaciation. Addison's disease prevents the body from producing enough adrenalin when needed for extra energy. Kennedy was controlling the condition with cortisone shots but took extra shots on days of higher tension.

In Vienna, Khrushchev came out swinging, so to speak, doing his best to intimidate the new president, about 20 years younger than the Soviet leader. Kennedy complained about Soviet subversion in the developing world. Khrushchev declared the Soviets were bound to eventually win the battle of ideas. Kennedy warned about the dangers of war by miscalculation, at which point the Soviet leader angrily responded that the Soviets do not make war by miscalculation.

The most ominous point of the meeting came near the end, when Khrushchev announced he was going to sign a peace treaty with East Germany in December. This was to be accompanied by guaranteeing the Western allies only six months of free access to West Berlin. This may have been the worst misunderstanding. Kennedy assumed that Khrushchev meant the West would be expelled after six months. Khrushchev most likely meant that the West would have to renegotiate with the East German government. Fortunately, for all concerned, the meeting ended soon after.

On the way back to Washington, Kennedy stopped in London to confer with British Prime Minister Harold Macmillan. He told Macmillan how badly the meeting had gone. Kennedy, however, sounded more optimistic a few days later when he spoke to the American people. He reported:

> I made it clear to Mr. Khrushchev that the security of Western Europe and therefore our own security are deeply involved in our presence and our access rights to West Berlin; that those rights are based on law not on sufferance; and that we are determined to maintain those rights at any risk and thus our obligation to the people of West Berlin and their right to choose their own future.[66]

Orbis, however, a journal of political analysis, did not think Kennedy had properly conveyed this message to the Soviets.

> ... Khrushchev… had good reason to doubt the West's resolution to stand firm in Berlin or elsewhere. It is not verbal warnings, but concrete measures which are likely to deter Khrushchev from dangerous miscalculations ... It is unlikely, therefore, that the Vienna meeting rebounded to the West's benefit ...[67]

Orbis was correct. On June 4, 1961, the Soviets issued a document demanding a four-power conference to come up with a final peace treaty for both Germanys and a final settlement of the Berlin issue. They were willing to accept another temporary settlement only for a limited and specific period. Should the West not agree to the Soviet conditions, the Soviets would sign a separate treaty with East Germany. The West would then have to negotiate access with East Germany. The Soviets were now going public with what Khrushchev had told Kennedy at their meeting.

Khrushchev saw Berlin as a point of Western vulnerability, a place where he could start and stop trouble when he saw advantages in doing so. Kennedy's errors at the Bay of Pigs and Vienna seemed to be presenting Khrushchev a target of opportunity for trouble. East Germany always made the Soviets insecure for the arbitrary border of their outer empire, with Berlin a Western outpost and potential crack in the empire's security.

THE BERLIN CRISIS OF 1961

The American response to the Soviet document was cleared with the European allies. There were some curious differences of opinion, with Great Britain favoring negotiation, France and West Germany wanting to stand firm. The United States finally decided to express a willingness to negotiate, but to refuse to do so under pressure. The official American reply declared that "with regard to Berlin, the United States ... is insisting on, and will defend, its legal rights against attempts at unilateral abrogation because the freedom of the people of West Berlin depends upon the maintenance of these rights ..."[68]

Kennedy spoke to the nation on July 25, 1961, stating the American intention not to back down over Berlin. His speech declared, "The endangered frontier of freedom runs through divided Berlin."[69] Leaders on both ends of the political spectrum, including Harry Truman and Richard Nixon, publicly supported his tough stand. A Gallup Poll indicated that 80 percent of the public was willing to risk war over Berlin. Concrete measures included sending a 1,500-man military force from West Germany to Berlin, accompanied by Vice President Lyndon Johnson. This move was allowed to pass. A scary postscript would occur in October of that year, with a brief face-off between American and Soviet tanks at the border. Both sides soon withdrew their forces.

The Berlin Crisis of 1961 was eased in an unusual manner. One noteworthy aspect of the Cold War was that a crisis would

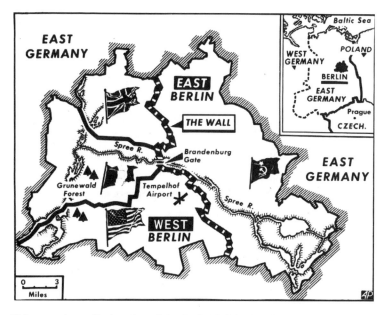

This map shows the location of the Berlin Wall in the divided city. The Brandenburg Gate was just barely inside the eastern sector of the city.

be solved not only by finding a way to back out without losing face but to enable an opponent to do the same thing. The Soviets found a way out to avoid being backed into a corner.

However it seemed to the public at the time, the underlying cause of the Berlin Crisis was not just Soviet bluster or Khrushchev playing power politics within his own government. The Iron Curtain effectively did not yet exist between East and West Berlin. People went back and forth daily in the hundreds of thousands. Sizable numbers of people, though, went across to West Berlin and stayed there. East Germany had border controls and tried increasingly to stop those fleeing. People with luggage got particular attention at the border, as did families traveling together. Refugees could work around both these problems. The creators of a security-based arbitrary border could not continue to tolerate its effective nonexistence in one key location, especially when this endangered a part of the total border important both militarily and economically to its creator.

Fleeing to West Berlin had some risk, though nothing close to the danger that would come in the later situation. Those who fled were people with more initiative. They also tended to be the more economically productive members of society, the better talented and educated, who anticipated not just freedom but being allowed to advance as far as they could in the West. Nearly 200,000 people fled East Germany in 1960, the population of a good-sized city. Not just a city, but also a very productive city, was leaving the country, never planning to return, every year. Khrushchev's aides, presumably not in their boss's presence, had been known to joke that "soon there will be no one left in the GDR except [Communist Party boss Walter] Ulbricht and his mistress."[70]

This emigration would risk virtually destroying the production capacity of East Germany. The East German government and their Soviet protectors-masters could not allow this to continue. The Soviets first tried bluff and bluster to get the Americans out. Harry Truman phrased it well, as quoted in the *New York Times,* when he said, "The Russians are the greatest bluffers in the history of the world. When their bluff is called they quit. Their bluff has been called by President Kennedy's speech. All we need to do is show them we mean business."[71] This remark was in keeping with the theory of Soviet behavior that had the Soviets probing for weakness and withdrawing if they did not find any. Bluffing or carrying out the threat to sign a unilateral treaty with East Germany, however, was risky in the nuclear era.

On Friday, August 11, 1961, 1,532 people fled East Berlin.[72] This number was actually down 200 from the day before. On Saturday, 2,662 people would flee. On Sunday, August 13, the East Germans began to carry out their solution to the refugee problem. Soon after midnight, the American mission in Berlin received a phone call, noting a considerable decrease in rapid rail traffic to the West. "The trains ran into the East and weren't coming back again. It created considerable confusion ..."[73] West Berlin taxi drivers were spreading the word to each other not to accept fares to the East. At the same time, on Cape Cod, John Kennedy was relaxing with his daughter and some friends, driving back on a golf cart from an ice cream parlor.

At a little after 1 A.M., a press office teletype began to clatter in an American news office in Berlin. A Warsaw Pact press release was coming over.

> The present traffic situation on the borders of West Berlin is being used by the ruling circles of West Germany and the intelligence agencies of the NATO countries to undermine the economy of the German Democratic Republic. Through deceit, bribery and blackmail, West German bodies and military interests induce certain unstable elements in the German Democratic Republic to leave for West Germany. In the face of the aggressive inspirations of the reactionary forces of West Germany and its NATO allies, the Warsaw Pact proposes reliable safeguards and effective control be established around the whole territory of West Berlin."[74]

The American journalist who received the message realized that the East Germans were closing the border. They were doing more. Ulbricht, despite his earlier statements, had gotten Soviet permission to build a wall. The wall actually started out as barbed wire emplacements, blocking off exits, with the actual wall constructed a few months later.

Another practice at the wall soon started. The afternoon the wall was started, a young boy talked his way across it. The guard who let him go was spotted and arrested for his troubles.

Most guards did not react so nicely. On August 19, 1961, Rudolf Urban fell from a building while trying to cross the wall. He died in the hospital about a week later. Five days later Gunter Litwan, 24, was shot by border guards while trying to cross. The last person shot and killed while trying to cross the wall died on February 5, 1989. The last accidental death, drowning in the canal on the border, occurred on April 16, 1989. In the 28-year history of the wall, 5,000 or so people managed to escape. This number was less than the weekly totals before the wall was built.

QUOTATIONS ABOUT THE BERLIN WALL

"West Berlin was becoming increasingly dangerous to the existence of the GDR and to the existence of socialism. Khrushchev proposed to create a free city of Berlin with special rights of its own. With its own foreign policy, its own police and its own symbolic foreign forces."

—Werner Eberlein, East German Interpreter

"The attempt to find a compromise with the Soviets was where we began to get into serious trouble, because any concessions that you made to the Soviets from the Western side would be an erosion of the Western position there and the Soviets themselves were committed to a situation in Berlin that the allies could not tolerate ... "

—Martha Mautner, U.S. State Department Intelligence

"A foreman in a plant in the East wouldn't know how many workers he still would have the next day because part of his working force had left him, had left the East, had left the system in order to go over there. Of course in West Germany they made every effort that people who came from the East would get jobs and would get a comfortable existence."

—Stefan Heym, East German Writer

"The [1961 Vienna summit] was unproductive and the longer it went on the more that became apparent. It was difficult, it was disappointing, it left us with a Berlin crisis that was still active and on which no progress had been made."

—McGeorge Bundy, aide to President Kennedy

"It is a fact that we were not going to fight about what the Soviets did on their side of Berlin and that it is quite likely that Khrushchev was helped to understand that American position by the July speech."

—McGeorge Bundy, aide to President Kennedy

"Everybody knew that something is going to happen. Not necessarily only from the atmosphere but for weeks thousands and thousands of people had come across and everybody realized that in some way or another, East Germany will have to react."

—Margit Hosseini, West German resident

"Sometime later a reply came back from Moscow that [Khrushchev] agrees to the closing of the border with West Germany and with West Berlin and suggests the necessary preparations should be carried out."

—Yuli Kvitsinski, Soviet Embassy, East Berlin

Some 250 were killed crossing the wall. There is no way to tell how many were discouraged from trying.

MEANING OF THE BERLIN WALL

The Berlin Wall will appear again in the story of the Cold War, providing some of the most unforgettable television images ever seen. Immediate reactions to the wall were different. The United States and its allies could do little. Primarily, the wall was entirely built on East German territory. The Western allies could complain about the wall dividing territory still technically under four-power control. In the real world, though, creating the artificial border of the Iron Curtain created East Germany as a real government, however questionable its long-term legitimacy or permanency. However negative it may make a government

"The people were swearing at us. We felt we were simply doing our duty but we were getting scolded from all sides. The West Berliners yelled at us and the Eastern demonstrators yelled at us. We were standing there in the middle. There was the barbed wire, there were us guards, West Berliners, East Berliners. For a young person, it was terrible."
—Conrad Schumann, East German border guard
(who defected to the West a day or two later)

"We were outraged and also disappointed. The mayor didn't manage to persuade the allied commanders to make even a small protest."
—Egon Bahr, West German politician

"They did it as a necessity and I thought, 'What kind of system is it that can only exist by keeping, by keeping them with force in their own bailiwick.' And the Wall was the actual symbol of a defeat, of inferiority."
—Stefan Heym, East German writer

"The Wall was a way out, really, for Khrushchev. And although the Berlin affair continued to be discussed, it was not, no longer in a state of crisis, as it had been before the Wall."
—Oleg Troyanovski, Khrushchev advisor

Source: CNN, Cold War Series, Script, Episode 9, "The Wall."

An East German officer (right) and a West German-U.S. Army officer face off across a line dividing East and West Berlin at the *Freidrichstrasse* checkpoint on October 16, 1961. They advanced and retreated on either side of a six-inch-wide white line painted across the street along what was supposed to be the precise border between East and West Berlin.

appear, a real government has the right to seal its borders. The West had to be content with protests and with using the wall as a physical example of the failures of European Communism.

The wall made things hard for the people of Berlin, particularly when it split families in half. This kind of difficulty is common with arbitrary borders, particularly when the border has no natural logic that would make it self-enforcing but rather has to be maintained by force. The conditions making East Germans want to leave certainly existed. Conditions did improve later, particularly after both Germanys began to deal with each other. Visits were allowed.

Construction of the Berlin Wall may well have prevented a war. The economic potential of East Germany was draining away across the border into West Germany. The East Germans and the Soviets could not have been expected to continue to tolerate the situation. Ideally, their system would not have caused the problem in the first place, but they stumbled on the best available way to solve it. In doing so, they provided the West with a powerful symbol of what was wrong with Communism.

6

Entangling Alliances

While the United States and Great Britain were defending part of their side of the Iron Curtain in Berlin in 1948, they were securing their whole side back in Washington, D.C. Negotiations for an Atlantic alliance involving Western Europe, Great Britain, and the United States continued during the Berlin airlift. The Soviet blockade, although it might have been partially motivated by the negotiations, spurred the parties on to get something settled. The preliminary Pentagon meetings, held before the Berlin blockade and airlift, got off to a good start, issuing a report with five recommendations:

1. The President of the United States would invite 13 other countries to join in negotiations. These countries were Great Britain, France, Canada, Belgium, Luxembourg, the Netherlands, Norway, Sweden, Denmark, Iceland, Ireland, Portugal, and Italy.

2. As a "stop-gap" until such an agreement was reached, the United States would guarantee the signatories of the Brussels Treaty (Great Britain, France, Luxembourg, the Netherlands, Belgium) against attack.

3. The United States would offer the same support to other nations joining the Brussels Treaty.

4. The United States and Great Britain would declare that they would not tolerate any threats to the independence or territorial integrity of Greece, Turkey, or Iran.

5. When circumstances allowed, Germany (or West Germany) would be invited to join the Brussels Treaty and the North Atlantic Treaty.

The Pentagon meetings agreed that the pattern for the proposed treaty would be the recently concluded Rio Treaty, signed by the nations of the Western Hemisphere, including the United States. This treaty regarded an attack on any member from anyone as an attack on all.

Interestingly, a British report on the proposed North Atlantic Treaty warned that the Pentagon recommendations were only recommendations, not guarantees of approvals by higher officials.

Much depended, the report said, on the Soviets' maintaining the tense climate. The Soviets, though likely informed through their agents of the recommendations the same time they were released, obliged. The same day the meetings ended, April 1, 1948, the preliminary moves of the Berlin blockade took place.

BIPARTISANSHIP IN THE UNITED STATES

Another factor affecting negotiations was the upcoming American presidential election—though election campaigns in the 1940s were not the nearly continuous affairs of today. Truman would be running for reelection on his own, not as Franklin Roosevelt's running mate. The Republicans controlling the Congress, particularly Senate Foreign Affairs Committee Chairman Arthur Vandenberg, wanted to cooperate with Truman but also wanted credit in an election year. Vandenberg was also a long-shot choice for the Republican nomination for President at their convention in July. Domestic political realities always affect foreign policy.

Vandenberg had been an isolationist before World War II. By his own admission, the Japanese attack on Pearl Harbor and the entry of the United States into the war changed his views. After the war, particularly after the Republicans took over the Congress in the election of 1946, Vandenberg became a firm supporter of the need for America to stay involved with the rest of the world. His support for particular measures, however, required either some trade-off from the administration or the freedom to take credit for the measure.

Under Secretary of State Robert Lovett was the administration's chief contact with Vandenberg. Lovett and Vandenberg decided the most realistic support the Congress could give was a resolution by the Senate that supported the general objectives of the North Atlantic Treaty negotiations, without referring to a still politically questionable formal alliance. The final resolution, which easily passed the Senate in early June, supported the development of regional "arrangements" for self-defense, in accordance with the United Nations charter. Vandenberg did not want to risk weakening the role of the United Nations, which he had expended political capital to support. The United States would associate itself with such arrangements in accordance with its constitutional procedures. This provision allowed for a treaty but did not specifically call for a treaty. The president would be able to interpret the resolution pretty much as he wished, subject to treaties requiring Senate approval.

The resolution passed on June 11, 1948. Nine days later, the Republican presidential nominating convention—what the Republicans hoped would be the first move in putting Harry Truman out of a job—opened in Philadelphia. Thomas Dewey, who had run against Roosevelt in 1944, got the Republican nomination on June 23, 1948. The next day, the Berlin Blockade began. Stalin apparently did not expect his actions in Berlin to risk war with the West, but he seemed to pay little attention to the possibility that Soviet actions would solidify the growing Western alliance.

Work toward the security treaty was already under way when the Berlin blockade and airlift began, though with little public attention. Kennan was still supporting effective guarantees of what the Americans would do in case of war in Europe rather than a formal alliance. On April 29, 1948, the Canadian Foreign Minister, Louis St. Laurent, speaking before the Canadian House of Commons called for "appropriate collective security arrangements."[75] Two weeks later, the Canadian ambassador to the United States had lunch with Kennan. The ambassador argued that it would be far easier for Canada and the United States to collaborate on defense planning within the framework of an overall treaty. This would make it easier for Canada to work with both Great Britain and the United States. It would also decrease difficulties associated with the fear of U.S. impingement on Canadian sovereignty. Further arguments were offered when Kennan was invited to Ottawa a few weeks later. Kennan was not really converted but gave in to what he saw as an inevitable treaty.

At about the same time, in response to an American request, the five members of the Brussels Treaty issued a statement

On August 24, 1949, President Harry S. Truman signed the North Atlantic Security Pact creating the North Atlantic Treaty Organization (NATO) as foreign diplomats and American officals looked on.

declaring their intent to resist any Soviet attack as far to the east as possible. They recognized the need to link their plans to American strategic and operational plans. The members of the Brussels Treaty may not have liked the increasingly strong arbitrary border between Western and Eastern Europe, but they intended to stay on the Western side.

FORMAL NATO TALKS OPEN

Formal negotiations for an Atlantic military alliance began in Washington on July 6, 1948. The weather was that of a typical Washington, D.C., summer day—hot and muggy. It was also before the days of common air conditioning, so many people, including those from government, media, and the diplomatic corps, would be out of town to avoid the heat. Pact supporters realized the need to eventually build public support for the

NATO MEMBERSHIP
Countries Negotiating the Treaty

Belgium
Canada
France
Great Britain
Luxembourg
The Netherlands
United States

Additional Countries Signing Treaty at Creation

Denmark
Iceland
Italy
Norway
Portugal

Joined in 1952

Greece
Turkey

Joined in 1955

Germany (then West Germany)

Joined in 1999

Czech Republic
Hungary
Poland

Expected to Join by May 2004

Bulgaria
Estonia
Latvia
Lithuania
Romania
Slovakia
Slovenia

Sources: NATO Handbook; NATO Web site at <www.nato.int>.

proposed alliance. The Pentagon Recommendations had said "That steps be taken to see that [the] ... significance of a possible North Atlantic Security Pact be made available for background to all higher officials of the Department, to Missions in the field, and to the informational organs of this Department and other Government Departments, with a view to keeping it before the public and to combat opposing concepts."[76]

The State Department wanted to downplay the negotiations and only announced talks on implementing the Vandenberg resolutions. Robert Lovett warned the ambassadors from France, Great Britain, Canada, Belgium, Holland, and Luxembourg that any leak at all, particularly during an American presidential election campaign, could spoil the whole thing. There is no indication what Soviet agent Donald Maclean, attending until August, thought.

The first five days were run like a type of ambassadors' working group, and accomplished little that was specific. The discussions were general, designed just to give some idea of the security and political situation in Europe and to estimate Soviet intentions. Possible solutions were discussed, including different ways the United States might relate to the new security arrangements. The French talked about the need for immediate American assistance for the Brussels Treaty states. The British and Canadian representatives, on the other hand, spoke of the need for a new arrangement, not just an expansion of the Brussels Treaty.

The one decision made at the initial meetings was to establish a working group of lower-level diplomatic personnel from the U.S. State Department and the embassies of the other six nations. This group began work almost immediately, on July 14, 1948.

THE WORKING GROUP

The Working Group, as it came to be called, met almost every working day until September. It was hot, so they worked informally in shirtsleeves. There soon developed an informal way of dealing with inevitable disagreements. The members all had instructions from their governments. If one country made a proposal the others did not like, they would talk and try to come up with a compromise. Whoever had instructions to the contrary would get them changed. No formal records were kept, so the participants could speak freely.

One thing that probably helped the discussions was that neither of the two primary State Department opponents of the treaty, George Kennan and Charles Bohlen, took part in all the discussions. Kennan was mostly an observer. Bohlen was a member but in September left Washington for the United Nations General Assembly meeting, being held in Paris because of the American election campaign. John D. Hickerson, from the State Department's European office and an early treaty supporter, was the leading American participant.

In mid-July, about the time the Working Group got under way, the foreign ministers of the Brussels Pact nations met in Holland to discuss the results of the Ambassador's Committee, which had created the Working Group. The French and Belgians were particularly bitter and accused the United States of trying to get out of any real commitment to Europe. British Foreign Secretary Bevin tried to restore calm to the meeting, pointing out that they all saw advantages to an Atlantic Pact. What Bevin knew, but the French did not know, was that despite seeming hesitation, the Americans were aiming at a viable treaty, one politically acceptable in the United States. This had been decided at secret meetings in Washington between the United States, Canada, and Great Britain.

Through a miscommunication, the French went into the discussions in Washington assuming they were to discuss American military aid for the Brussels Treaty. During the continuing talks, the French pressed for aid to such an extent that it might have wrecked the efforts at a treaty. In late August, Lester Pearson, then Canadian under secretary of external affairs and later prime minister, reported back to his government in Ottawa in two cables that "the attitude of the French is causing increasing impatience and irritation here and is incomprehensible to everybody." He later added, "These discussions demonstrated that the Americans are becoming profoundly impatient with the negative attitude of the French. There is, I think, a real danger of the whole project being wrecked."[77]

The French concern was about getting concrete assurances and aid when needed. This concern was finally addressed when Lester Pearson told the Canadian ambassador to France to remind the French that if they were that worried about an American commitment to send reinforcements to Europe, joint planning agencies under a treaty would make it impossible for the United States to refuse to give assurances of immediate ground forces aid if needed. This suggestion, along with the change of government in France, convinced the French to fully support a treaty. One may note a pattern since World War II that when the United States wants to stay somewhere, it is told to go home, and when it wants to go home, it is told to stay.

A few weeks later, in September 1948, Truman acted to reassure the French. He approved sending surplus American equipment to Germany to bring three French divisions up to combat readiness.

MORE AMERICAN POLITICAL REALITIES

All the involved parties were now looking toward a treaty and a formal military alliance. By early September, a Working Group report recommended and provided the case for a treaty. On September 9, 1948, the Ambassador's Committee gave its approval and sent it off to the various governments. The treaty text would still have to be negotiated, signed, and ratified by the involved nations. The die, however, was cast.

Another major event occurred two months later. On November 2, 1948, to the surprise of political pollsters, media, elected officials, and Thomas E. Dewey, the Republican candidate for President, Harry Truman was reelected president of the United States. The Democrats also regained control of both houses of Congress. This situation led to an interesting problem for Truman. When Congress returned in January 1949, Tom Connally of Texas would become chairman of the Senate Foreign Relations Committee. Connally was a loyal Democrat, but he was neither as astute nor as naturally international-minded as Vandenberg. Some political work would have to be done here.

Interestingly, one major domestic political issue would not plague treaty negotiations. The right wing of the Republican Party, getting ready, in a manner of speaking, for Joe McCarthy's Communist "witch hunts," would not be much of a problem. Even these Republicans realized they could not hunt Communists at home and oppose a treaty designed to stop Communists in Europe.

A second political change was that George Marshall resigned as secretary of state for reasons of health. Dean Acheson, who had previously served as number two in the State Department, replaced Marshall. Acheson was very experienced but not always as diplomatic as Marshall. Acheson would hold office for all of Truman's second term.

Some operational details for the treaty, the organization it would create, still had to be worked out. On April 9, 1949, however, the NATO Treaty was signed in Washington, D.C. The U.S. Senate ratified the treaty in July of that year. The process was eased by an incautious assurance by the administration that American troops would not have to be sent to Europe. About the time the treaty was announced, the Soviets dropped their first hints about ending the Berlin blockade.

The United States would appoint the military commander of all NATO forces, a practice still followed. This command needed an American military leader particularly skilled in diplomacy and in working with forces from different nations. The United States had such a man, Dwight Eisenhower. Eisenhower took over in April 1951 and served until resigning in September 1952 to run for president.

The busy year of 1949 had not ended. On May 24, 1949, the Basic Law of the Federal Republic of Germany went into effect.

This can be considered West German independence day. On September 13, 1949, the White House announced that the Soviet Union had exploded an atomic bomb. American intelligence had thought it would be several years before the Soviets would have the bomb. This, however, was before the exposure of extensive Soviet espionage efforts in the United States and Great Britain, particularly during World War II in the Manhattan Project, which was set up to create nuclear weapons. In January 1950, Truman ordered the U.S. military to begin development of the hydrogen bomb.

On October 1, 1949, Mao Zedong declared the Communist victory in the Chinese civil war by proclaiming the People's Republic of China. Communist victory had been expected for some months.

By this time, the idea of U.S. troops being sent to Europe was far more politically acceptable. The American people were recognizing the truth of something James Byrnes had said in Paris a few years before: "The people of the United States have discovered that when a European war starts, our own peace and security inevitably become involved before the finish. They have concluded that if they must help finish every European war, it would be better for them to do their part to prevent the starting of a European war."[78]

Surprisingly, the Warsaw Pact, considered the Communist counterpart to the NATO Treaty, was not signed until May 1955. The Soviets, however, already had defense treaties and agreements with the Eastern European countries. The Warsaw Pact formalized agreements already in effect, in response to West Germany's joining NATO a few days before. One can say that by January 1950, the "sides" for the Cold War were chosen. The arbitrary border of the Iron Curtain was set and would see no changes until 1989.

7

Interrelationships —Hungary and Suez

With the dangerous exception of Berlin, where the last confrontation occurred in 1961, active competition in the Cold War occurred outside the European Central Front, out of sight of the Iron Curtain. Superpower competition occurred in fringe areas, with proxy forces on at least one side, where they were less likely to escalate to disastrous proportions. The Korean War, which began the 1950s, was one such "outside" conflict, which both sides managed to contain. The Iron Curtain may have been arbitrary, but its stability was also seen as protective.

Less drastically than Korea, by the mid-1950s the developing world, the so-called third world, was becoming the primary area for Cold War competition. The main European colonial powers, Great Britain and France, were granting independence to and withdrawing from their colonies. Both sides in the Cold War saw these new countries as areas where they could expand their influence. President Eisenhower recognized this. He declared in his second inaugural address, January 20, 1956, that "New forces and new nations stir and strive across the Earth.... one-third of all mankind has entered upon an historic struggle for a new freedom: freedom from grinding poverty ... Not even America's prosperity could long survive if other nations did not long prosper."[79]

John Foster Dulles, secretary of state during most of Eisenhower's time in office, was the chief supporter of the idea of "rolling back" Communist influence. Appealing in theory, the idea of freeing nations from oppressive Soviet dominance would have been dangerously destabilizing in the real world of Europe. The Soviets also looked outside Europe for an area in which to expand their influence. The developing world seemed made to order. Resentment of the recently departed colonial powers, which transferred to resentment of their ally the United States, tended to make the Soviet system seem attractive.

The leaders of the third world saw the ideological conflict between the "superpowers" (a term beginning to be applied to the United States and the Soviet Union) as an opportunity to help their nations and, unfortunately, sometimes themselves.

In June 1955, Gamel Abdul Nasser attempted to set up the Bandung, Indonesia conference, which was the first major attempt to establish the nonaligned countries as a political force. Nasser was in power at the time the Suez Canal was nationalized in 1956— that is, control of the canal was taken over by the Egyptians.

Some nonaligned leaders, including independent Communists such as the Yugoslavians and, after the split with the Soviet Union, China, tried to establish a third force. The leaders wanted to play the United States and Soviet Union against each other, in effect forcing them to bid for influence.

One of the more influential nonaligned leaders was Egypt's Gamel Abdul Nasser. Nasser came to power as an indirect result of the 1948–1949 Israeli war of independence. About a year after the British handed over the Palestine mandate to the United Nations, as one of the "secondary" money-saving moves that included ending aid to Greece, the Jewish population of Palestine declared the independent state of Israel. Their five closest Arab neighbors—Egypt, Jordan, Syria, Lebanon, and Iraq— immediately invaded. The badly outnumbered Israelis repulsed the Arab armies, gaining some territory, losing other territory. For the Israelis and for the generally sympathetic West, particularly the United States, this was a good thing. For the Arabs, this was *al-Nakbah,* the disaster.[80] They had bungled, in their eyes, their first major post-colonial operation.

For the Soviets, it was an opportunity. Nikita Khrushchev would later say of Israel that "Deserving of condemnation [is] ... the State of Israel, which from the first days of its existence began to threaten its neighbors."[81] The Soviets quickly realized that Israel, though starting out as a socialist state, was also democratic. They lost interest in supporting Zionism, in presenting it as an anticolonial movement, when the colonial powers withdrew from the Middle East. It was more useful to oppose Zionism as colonial and a tool of the imperialists. The Soviets would await their chance to take advantage of their opportunity in the Middle East.

Nasser and the West would provide them with this opportunity. In 1952, Nasser was a 34-year-old lieutenant colonel in the Egyptian army. He became one of the leaders who overthrew King Farouk. About a year later, Nasser emerged from the pack to become "the first true Egyptian to rule Egypt since the Persian conquest nearly two thousand five hundred years before."[82] Whatever other elements made up Nasser's character, independent nationalism was always there. Nasser, interestingly, was initially not as active against Israel as one would think. He kept the Suez Canal closed to Israeli shipping and sponsored some Palestinian guerrilla raids into Israel, but he seemed to be keeping the "Israeli issue" on the back burner, to use a modern political phrase. Public opinion, a factor even in repressive regimes, however, was not satisfied. Furthermore, the Israelis began to retaliate for the raids.

In June 1955, Nasser took time out to help set up the Bandung, Indonesia, conference, the first major attempt to establish the nonaligned world as a political force. Interestingly, the People's Republic of China attended the meeting, perhaps anticipating the upcoming split with the Soviets and seeking additional areas of support and influence. The United States would never really accept the idea of nonalignment in the Cold War. The Soviets were a little subtler in holding much the same position.

Nasser responded to the Israeli retaliations in September 1955 with a massive purchase of Soviet arms through Czechoslovakia. Nasser began to use the arms almost immediately, with the six months after the purchase seeing expanded cross-border fighting with Israel. Israeli Prime Minister David Ben Gurion saw the need for a showdown with Egypt and began looking for a major power ally. The United States was still hoping to compete with the Soviets to influence the Arabs, so it refused, as did Great Britain. France agreed.

Several other issues then intervened. On July 19, 1956, believing that Nasser was becoming too friendly with the Communists (though never enough to legalize the Communist Party in Egypt), Secretary of State John Foster Dulles announced that the United States would not fund the proposed dam on the Nile River. The Soviets would eventually finance the dam. Seven days later, Nasser nationalized the Suez Canal, seizing control from the British-French group running the canal.

Events in proximity to the Iron Curtain began to intermix with those in the Middle East. In early October, labor problems in Poland were settled peacefully. Khrushchev's speech to the Twentieth Communist Party Congress in the spring of 1956, meant to be secret but obtained by Israeli intelligence, had provoked expectation in Eastern Europe of general Soviet liberalization. The expectation, though, was further than Khrushchev was prepared to go. Problems in Poland were settled peacefully, but problems in other areas behind the Iron Curtain would not work out so well.

TWIN CRISES

About the same time Poland was calming down, Dulles warned Great Britain and France that defending the Suez Canal was not part of the American obligation to her allies. On October 22–24, 1956, British, French, and Israeli military leaders met secretly in France. They planned to have Israel stage an attack

One of the "casualties" of the student demonstrations in Budapest, Hungary was a large statue of Joseph Stalin that was pulled down to the ground by demonstrators. The large statue was later taken away from where it had stood in front of the National Theater and smashed into pieces by the people.

toward the Suez Canal, but with the main Israeli effort directed at opening the Straits of Tiran, which led to Israel's southern port of Eilat. Great Britain and France would then demand that Israel and Egypt withdraw from the canal. When Egypt refused, British and French troops would occupy the canal.

The day before the meeting ended, student demonstrations broke out in Budapest, Hungary. Police attempts to disperse the crowd turned the demonstration into a riot. Martial law was declared, and the Hungarian government asked for Soviet assistance. Soviet troops entered Budapest that night. The next day, Imre Nagy, a reform-minded leader removed as premier in 1955, again became premier. On October 25, with fighting continuing in Budapest, Janos Kadar became head of the Communist Party.

Early in the morning of October 29, Israeli forces attacked into the Sinai Desert. Paratroops captured the Mitla Pass that day, 24 miles from the Suez Canal. The next day, Israel accepted the British-French ultimatum to withdraw, though Egypt, as predicted (and hoped), refused. The same day, in Budapest, Nagy announced the end of the one-party system in Hungary and the start of negotiations for the withdrawal of Soviet troops.

On October 31, British planes bombed Egyptian airfields. The next day, Nagy made what turned out to be his fatal move. He announced that Hungary was withdrawing from the Warsaw Pact and would become neutral. (Some experts considered this the Nagy government's worst mistake.) Nagy asked that the Hungarian question be considered by the United Nations. Soviet troops began to move back toward Budapest. The same day, moving substantially faster than Great Britain and France had expected, Israel's military units reached the west bank of the Suez Canal. It had taken 100 hours. British armored units were still making their leisurely way to Egypt by sea.

November 3 saw more government changes in Hungary, with many non-Communist ministers joining the government. This proved too much for the Soviets.

Khrushchev was already concerned about events in Hungary, both the practical effects of letting the Hungarians go their own way and the image presented to the West. He told Tito, "If we let things take their course [in Hungary] then the West will say we are either stupid or weak and that's one and the same thing."[83]

On November 4, at the urging of their ambassador to Hungary, Yuri Andropov, Soviet troops attacked Budapest. Nagy was overthrown and took shelter in the Yugoslavian embassy. Fighting took several days and killed an estimated 3,000 Hungarians. Many more fled the country. Nagy was eventually tricked out of the embassy by promises of safe conduct, captured, and executed.

The Hungarians hoped for assistance from the West, consistent with the roll-back doctrine. On November 4, 1956, at the height of the Soviet attacks on Budapest, a Hungarian cabinet minister broadcast, "I appeal to the great powers of the world for a wise and courageous decision in the interest of my enslaved nation and of the liberty of all Eastern European nations."[84] American aid was never a realistic possibility. Eisenhower knew this, and he turned down CIA requests to airdrop arms.

This decision was cynical on Eisenhower's part, perhaps, but also realistic. Probably without even thinking about it, both sides had come to prefer an effective freeze on conditions in proximity of the Iron Curtain. The concept of arbitrary borders implies creation without regard to their effect on local realities. A recurring theme in the history of the Cold War in Europe, however, is that the arbitrary border of the Iron Curtain had taken on an almost perverse logic. Peaceful stability resulted from the Iron Curtain. Change could bring on an alternative far worse. Both sides could also console themselves with philosophical beliefs that the other's system would eventually collapse.

British and French paratroops landed in Egypt the same day. Sea forces finally arrived the next day. On November 6, the British and French finally gave in to sharp American criticism and Soviet threats, and they agreed to withdraw. Israel took several more months to agree. That same day, Eisenhower overwhelmingly won reelection.

A day or so after his reelection, Eisenhower received a message from Nicolai Bulganin, chairman of the Presidium of the USSR Council of Ministers, that "I feel urged to state that the problem of withdrawal of Soviet troops from Hungary ... comes completely and entirely under the competence of the Hungarian and Soviet governments."[85] Eisenhower recognized the implications of what Bulganin was saying, that the Iron Curtain had effectively divided Europe into spheres of influence. Short of full-scale war, the United States could not do anything.

FOLLOW-UPS

Hungary would next appear in the news in 1989. Janos Kadar, however, proved to be a more moderate leader than expected from someone who had come to power as a clear Soviet tool.

The Middle East would remain in the news. Objectively, the

Nasser military lost in 1956. Nasser's survival, however, proved a political victory. British and French relationships with the United States were damaged. Some sources have said that the relationship with France was never the same after this episode. Israel and Egypt continued to be a front burner issue for another two decades.

In 1967, things heated up again. Soviet intelligence reported to Egypt, incorrectly, that Israel was planning an attack on Syria in retaliation for Syrian shelling of Israeli settlements. One theory is that this was a pure error on the part of the Soviets. Another is that it was intentional, part of a Kremlin power play over the appointment of a new head of the KGB, the Soviet international spy agency. The Vietnam War, then nearing its height, was seen as diverting American attention from the Middle East.

Nasser felt himself under heavy political pressure to act in some way to help Syria. He did so by shutting the Straits of Tiran, which lead from the Red Sea, to Israeli shipping to Eilat. The Israelis spent the next weeks trying to get international assistance in opening the straits. No one would act, however. Near the end of May, Nasser demanded that the United Nations withdraw its peacekeepers, in place in Sinai and Gaza since 1956. Nasser likely expected that United Nations Secretary-General U Thant would refuse. Nasser had been undecided about how to react to the apparent threat to Syria. At one point, he was less than an hour away from striking the first blow and initiating war with Israel. He backed away, though, and may well have intended the threatened withdrawal of UN troops as, basically, a bluff.

Israel, however, had no choice but to assume Nasser was playing for keeps. They could reach this conclusion just by listening to Nasser. In May, after closing the Straits of Tiran, Nasser told a convention of Arab trade unionists, "We knew that the closing of the Gulf of Aqaba meant war with Israel. If war comes it will be total and the objective will be Israel's destruction..."[86] Even if this is not what he really intended, Nasser could get caught up in his own rhetoric and pressure from the proverbial "street." One Egyptian official commented that "I now understand that the

streets of Cairo reflected the concept that had seized the leadership, namely that the destruction of Israel was a child's game
that only required the hooking up of a few telephone lines at the
commander's house and the writing of victory slogans."[87]

Thant agreed to withdraw the United Nations troops on May
19, just a day or two after Nasser's request. In the next few weeks,
the Israelis realized that diplomatic efforts were not going to
work. Just after dawn on Monday, June 6, 1967, as Egyptian
pilots were sitting down to breakfast after morning patrols, the
Israeli airforce staged a massive attack on Egyptian airfields.
Within a few hours, they had virtually destroyed the Egyptian
airfields. Later that day, in response to shelling from Jordan and
some air attacks, the Israelis destroyed the Jordanian, Iraqi, and
Syrian airfields. By Saturday, June 10, the Israelis had occupied
the Sinai Peninsula, the West Bank of the Jordan River, Gaza, and
the Golan Heights, at least twice as much territory as in Israel
proper before the war began. They then accepted the United
Nations Security Council Resolution calling for a cease-fire.

The Soviet Union was outraged at the Israeli attack. The
United States was sympathetic. Neither side intervened, however, aside from sponsoring the UN resolutions to end the fighting. The Soviets would make up Arab losses. The United States
would become Israel's chief ally and arms supplier.

The Soviet Union, accidentally or otherwise, helped provoke
the 1967 war. The 1973 war between Israel and Egypt and Syria,
on the other hand, was made possible when Nasser's successor,
Anwar Sadat (Nasser had died in 1971), threw out Soviet advisors. Despite striking first, the Egyptians were on the verge of an
even worse defeat when the United Nations stopped the fighting.
Sadat tried a different method in 1978, when Egypt became the
first Arab state to sign a peace treaty with Israel. Sadat himself
was murdered in 1981. Israeli-Egyptian relations cannot be
described as friendly, but there has been no war.

With the signing of the peace treaty with Egypt and many
years later with Jordan, these borders became relatively secure.
One can say they became real rather than just arbitrary. An

uneasy stability has existed on the Golan Heights between Israel and Syria. The West Bank and the Gaza Strip, as well as the border with Palestinian-controlled areas of southern Lebanon, have proven to be far more troublesome and remain so at the time this book went to press.

8

The Short
Prague Spring

At the end of 1968, a joke was circulating in Czechoslovakia: "Every Czech knows what is the luckiest country in the world: Israel, because it is surrounded by enemies."[88]

This cynical sense of humor was earned. In 1938 and 1939, Czechoslovakia was the victim of the British and French failure to understand Adolf Hitler and their unreadiness for war. In 1948, the country did not actually vanish from the map. Its effective independence and freedom of action, however, was a victim of Joseph Stalin's desire to secure his control of the areas to the east of the Iron Curtain. A few years later, the very Communist leaders who destroyed Czech democracy were themselves destroyed in Stalin's purges undertaken in reaction to Tito's break. By 1968, Czechoslovakia was considered so firmly in the Soviet camp that no Soviet troops were stationed on its territory.

In late 1967, Prague police used tear gas to break up a peaceful protest. This was shortly before the start of a party congress. This congress and the backlash from the protest resulted in the resignation of Antoine Novotny as head of the Communist Party in January 1968 and as president in March. Ludvig Svoboda became president. The obscure first secretary of the Slovak Communist Party became head of the Czechoslovakian Party. This was Alexander Dubcek.

THE PRAGUE SPRING BEGINS

Soon after he took over, after he consolidated his power, it became apparent that Dubcek was not the usual Communist leader. The "Action Program," released in April 1968, was the start of the Czech attempt to introduce a new attitude toward government, "socialism with a human face." Dubcek and his government, though not actually responsible to anyone but themselves, would act as though they were responsible to the people. The Soviet Union and most of the other Warsaw Pact allies did not react well to these proposed changes. They believed that Dubcek's reforms, meant to improve the lot of his people, were endangering the role of the Communist Party in Czechoslovakia. If such reforms could happen there, they might

Alexander Dubcek became the leader of the Czechoslovakian Communist Party in 1968 and introduced a style of government that seemed to be more responsive to the people. Unfortunately, the Soviet authorities believed that Dubcek's reforms were endangering the party's supremacy.

happen in the other nations of the Warsaw Pact or in the Soviet Union itself.

In viewing the events of 20 years later, one issue to consider is whether the Soviets were correct in this concern. Did liberalization destroy Communism in the Soviet Union and the rest of Eastern Europe? Or would better Soviet leadership have found a way to repair their system?

This was in the future, however. In 1968, Dubcek and his associates faced an increasing campaign of harassment from the Soviets. In May, the Soviets began to apply pressure. The campaign began with editorials and hostile propaganda and then led into threatening troop maneuvers. The next step seemed uncertain as late as July 1968, when the Kremlin seemed content with nasty notes. One such note read, in part,

> We cannot agree that enemy forces should divert your country from the path of Socialism and expose Czechoslovakia to

the danger of being torn from the socialist community. This is
no longer your affair alone. This is the affair of all Communist
and workers' parties ... There are forces in Czechoslovakia
capable of defending the socialist system ...[and these forces
can count on the] solidarity and all-around support from fraternal socialist countries."[89]

Newsweek had a major article on Prague in its July 29, 1968,
issue. The article, in addition to reporting on Soviet pressure,
such as the note quoted above, speculated that the Soviets had
two realistic options. One was to let reforms run their course,
trusting that Dubcek would keep Czechoslovakia ideologically
and militarily loyal to the Soviet Union. A free non-Communist
Czechoslovakia, however, *Newsweek* went on to say, "poses grave
strategic problems for the Soviet Union, since it would crack the
buffer zone that the Russians have constructed around the
periphery of their country following World War II ..."[90]
Newsweek also discussed the political risks of the second alternative, what use of force would do to the Soviet Union's image
and its relationship with the West.

The Soviets were willing to take these risks precisely for the
reason *Newsweek* gave. The Iron Curtain, the arbitrary border
dividing Europe, was seen as a protective buffer for the Soviet
Union. On July 29, the Soviet leadership met with the Czech
leadership outside Prague. Major Soviet military maneuvers
took place at the same time. Some of these maneuvers involved
Soviet troops in East Germany and Poland moving toward the
Czech border. By the third day of the talks, however, the Soviets
saw that bluster was not working. At one point during the meeting, with Soviet Party leader Leonid Brezhnev conveniently "ill"
and out of the room, some other members of the Soviet delegation accused Dubcek of having "imperialist agents" in the senior
Czech leadership. Dubcek responded by saying, "If you really
believe that there are Imperialist agents among the leaders of the
Czechoslovak Communist Party, then there is no point in continuing these talks."[91] Dubcek then left the meeting.

Sometime that day Brezhnev received letters from Tito of Yugoslavia as well as the leaders of the French and Italian Communists parties saying they would not support continued efforts to browbeat Czechoslovakia. The talks seemed to end in compromise. Dubcek spoke on television to announce that reforms would continue but within socialism. He also pledged that his nation's army "is a firm link in the Warsaw Pact and a sufficient guarantee for the protection of our borders."[92] Dubcek realized that the Soviets were particularly sensitive over the fact that Czechoslovakia was the only Warsaw Pact nation to border on the Soviet Union and West Germany and had been used as an invasion jumping-off point in Operation Barbarossa, in June 1941. He thought it sufficient to reassure the Soviets that his country would not become a threat and could defend against West Germany. A second meeting with the Soviets, to which the Warsaw Pact leaders had been invited a few days later seemed to confirm that the Prague Spring could continue.

AUGUST 21, 1968

Alexander Dubcek received word very late at night on August 20, 1968, that foreign troops had violated the real Czech borders. He thought that either some troops on maneuver had accidentally crossed or that this was a provocation to get the Czech army to fight, to which the Soviets would respond with a real invasion. Dubcek could not imagine the Soviets would be breaking their agreement of only a few days before.

The next morning, August 21, a Soviet embassy car and several armored cars drove into the square beneath Dubeck's window. Soviet soldiers and KGB men jumped out of the car. A Czech nearby shouted some insults and was shot dead. Dubcek now realized what was happening and picked up a phone to call the Soviet ambassador but could not get through. The Soviets burst into the room where Dubcek and some senior associates were sitting. The Soviets cut the phone lines and then arrested all the Czech officials. After being put into the armored cars, they were hog-tied, bent backward with their hands tied to their feet.

A Czechoslovakian student defiantly waves the nation's flag while standing on a Soviet tank during the Soviet-led invasion and occupation of Prague on August 22, 1968.

The leaders were eventually taken to a town in the Ukraine, and held there. Apparently, their guards were awaiting word that a successor government had been formed. Once they were no longer needed, the Czech leaders would likely have been executed.[93]

The new government was formed and announced but never began work. Massive protests occurred in Prague and soon throughout the rest of the country, requiring Soviet force and making it impossible for the government to function. Czechoslovak students had been required to take Russian in school, so they were able to insult the Russian troops in Russian. Road signs were changed, except for those pointing the way back to Moscow; they remained accurate. At one point, in Bratislava, someone warned a tank crew that the water supply had been poisoned. The Soviet soldiers ended up taking water from the very polluted Danube River, with predictable stomach problems.

The Soviets were having problems with their public image, but back in 1968 this was not a major concern. While the demonstrations were going on, Dubcek and the other Czechoslovakian leaders were with the Soviet leaders, but this time not from anything close to a position of equality. The Soviets were talking; the Czechs had no choice but to listen. The Soviets were telling them to undo virtually every reform, to plunge Czechoslovakia back to the repressive quiet of a year before. Plus, the Soviets also won agreement to station Soviet troops on Czechoslovak territory, allegedly to defend against West Germany but also to be on the scene to prevent another attempt at liberalization. Dubcek and associates were soon removed from power. They were lucky to have escaped with their lives.

SOVIET-WESTERN RELATIONS AFTER THE PRAGUE SPRING

The Soviet leadership likely calculated that whatever problems invading Czechoslovakia would cause for their relationship with the West, particularly with the United States, it would not last long. They were correct. The realities of the Iron Curtain and nuclear weapons made the West as powerless to help in Prague in 1968 as the West had been to help in Budapest in 1956. Relations were chilly for a while, through what was left of Lyndon Johnson's term. The people of Czechoslovakia settled back for 20 years of dull Communist repression, sinking below the Western radar.

A new American president took office in January 1969, Richard Nixon. Nixon came to office with strong anti-Communist credentials. He brought with him a national security advisor, Henry Kissinger, who later become secretary of state. Kissinger was a believer in old-fashioned balance of power and in the need to get along with the Soviet Union. The era of détente began. One of the main pillars of détente was the continuing effort to sign treaties limiting nuclear weapons and to confirm Cold War borders. The major diplomatic achievement of this period was the 1972 treaty effectively banning defensive systems in an effort to stop production of nuclear missiles.

Détente survived Nixon's resignation in 1974 and his replacement by Vice President Gerald Ford. It survived Ford's defeat in 1976 by Jimmy Carter. It did not survive the Soviet invasion of Afghanistan in 1979 to defend a Communist regime—one that had overthrown another Communist regime. Détente slipped into the "evil empire" days in 1981, when Ronald Reagan, having defeated Jimmy Carter in his run for reelection, took office. Reagan's idea seems to have been to bankrupt the Soviet Union by expanding the arms race. Whether the Soviet economy could compete with the West had always been a consideration for American policymakers. Could the Soviets keep up, or would the system eventually collapse?

Reagan was criticized for being excessively confrontational with the Soviets, for failing to reach out to their leadership. To which leaders, though? Leonid Brezhnev died in 1982. His successor, Yuri Andropov, died in 1983. Andropov's successor, Konstanin Chernenko, died in early 1985. He was replaced by Mikhail Gorbachev.

WHY INVASION?

Soon after "settling" things with Czechoslovakia, the Soviets turned their verbal guns on another Eastern European problem, Romania. There was serious concern in the West that, having taken the political "hit" for Czechoslovakia, the Soviets would use the new "Brezhnev doctrine," the right to interfere in all Communist states, to take care of all their problems at once. Romania was not attacked, however, and the reasons had to do with the same reasons the Prague Spring was brought to a violent halt.

Czechoslovakia occupies a central place in Europe. Czechoslovakia was the only country to border on West Germany and the Soviet Union. The mountains in the west were considered excellent defensive territory. Czechoslovakia was seen as a major part of the "Northern tier" of defenses and buffer of

Soviet territory. The territories of the members of the Warsaw Pact, particularly those that bordered directly on the Soviet Union, served as a defense perimeter. In crushing the Prague Spring, the Soviet Union gave notice that it would not risk change in the artificial border central to the Cold War.

A nation's defense is, and must be, of primary concern to the nation. At its height, the Soviet Union, however, disregarded the interests of its satellites in order to protect itself. It saw the function of the Warsaw Pact "allies" as complete subservience to Soviet needs. Whatever the political damage this would cause and whatever the offense against conventional morality, its practical value was questionable. A country can neutralize another country as a threat, but can it make the other country be an ally just by drawing a border? During the Cold War, some Western experts, for example, wondered if the Polish army would not only fail to fight for the Soviets but would turn on the Soviets and effectively become a NATO ally.

Invading Czechoslovakia was the Soviets' way of conveying a warning that their security, even their sense of security, came before the liberty and welfare and even the lives of the people of Eastern Europe. The invasion was meant as warning to the other members of the Warsaw Pact and the nearby nations to neither act nor even appear to be acting in a way that might possibly run counter to the Soviet idea of collective security or the Soviet impression of its own security needs.

Czechoslovakia, however, which was invaded, had sworn it would remain part of the Warsaw Pact. Romania, which was not invaded, had left the pact. How can one explain this difference?

One way is that either the Soviets did not believe the Dubcek government or that they just could not afford to take a chance. Romania borders on the Soviet Union but also on Hungary, Bulgaria, and Yugoslavia, not one of which was considered a military threat. Yugoslavia and the pro-Chinese Albania do not border on the Soviet Union. None of those countries could be as damaging. A Czechoslovakia less than 100 percent devoted to the Soviet Union and its system seemed to the Soviets to provide too much of a risk of creating a hole in the Soviet's defensive sphere, the sphere represented by the artificial border called the Iron Curtain.

Despite its noisy independence, Romania was much more repressive than the Soviet Union itself. This may explain why Romania escaped invasion and Czechoslovakia did not. In 1968, the Soviets did not wish to border on any socialist state being run as anything resembling a democracy. Such a nation, even if providing no danger to the arbitrary security border, would seem to endanger the arbitrary ideological border. It would stand as a bad example, from the Soviet point of view, to the Soviet people.

How could the Kremlin continue to say that the Soviet command style of government was necessary to achieve socialism when a country just across the border was letting its citizens have a voice in running their own affairs? This was intolerable and explains why the Soviet Union considered how its neighbors ran their internal policies to be more important than their foreign policy, as long as the foreign policy was not actively anti-Soviet. The final chapter of this book makes clear whether the Soviet fear of reform was justified.

9

1989—The End of an Era

Historians cite different events and dates for the beginning of the Cold War between the United States and the Soviet Union. The favorite seems to be the February 1945 Yalta Conference, when Franklin Roosevelt and Winston Churchill either "sold out" to the Soviets, or recognized and accepted political realities, as the start of the creation of the arbitrary border known as the Iron Curtain. Others prefer 1946, with Stalin's speech "declaring" cold war, Churchill's "Iron Curtain" speech answering the declaration, and George Kennan's "Long Telegram" explaining the West's adversary and suggesting ways of handling this adversary. Historians and commentators agree, however, on the end of the Cold War—1989. The 1991 collapse of the Soviet Union, following the bungled coup against Mikhail Gorbachev, is considered just an aftershock, scary for a few days until people realized the full degree of incompetence of the coup plotters, "the gang that couldn't coup straight."

What is interesting about 1989, however, is that politically it did not begin on January 1, 1989, whatever the calendar said. Some think it began in March 1985, when Gorbachev came to power in the Soviet Union with the goal of changing and improving his country. Others argue it began on December 25, 1979, twelve years to the day before Gorbachev resigned, when the Soviets invaded Afghanistan. For the first time, the Brezhnev Doctrine, the right to intervene in socialist states, was being used outside the Soviet's "sphere of influence" in Eastern Europe.

The Soviet invasion of Afghanistan led to a sharp reversal in President Jimmy Carter's attitude toward the Soviets. Carter began to strengthen the U.S. military; a process speeded up by Ronald Reagan. Reagan already considered the Soviet Union an "evil empire." Afghanistan gave him a reason. Reagan's arms buildup is credited with damaging, if not destroying, the weaker Soviet economy as the Soviets strained to keep up. Whatever the accuracy of Reagan's theory, which even now can probably never be proven, as far back as Kennan, observers had speculated about basic weaknesses in the Soviet system that, given the right type of pressure—a major continuing strain but not an obvious

A soldier in the Soviet Army takes down the Soviet flag at an airbase in Kabul, Afghanistan in January 1989 as the Soviets made their final troop withdrawal from that war-torn country.

threat to Soviet survival or Russian patriotism—could bring about a collapse of that system.

"All the wars that Russia lost led to social reform, while all of the wars it won led to the strengthening of totalitarianism,"[94] a perceptive Soviet general commented soon after the war in Afghanistan ended. The Soviets had suffered about 10,000 casualties by February 15, 1989. On that day, the last Soviet commander, Lieutenant-General Boris Gromov, clad in combat fatigues, walked over a bridge back onto Soviet soil, the symbolic last Soviet soldier in Afghanistan. Anti-Soviet elements in this country, and the government agencies that helped finance the war against the Soviets, might not have been so happy if they could have anticipated the Taliban taking control of the country a few years later and the chain of events leading to the September 11, 2001, terrorist attacks. This drastic example of the law of unintended consequences, however, was in the future; the amazing 1989 still had to unfold.

GLASNOST AND PERESTROIKA

Glasnost and *perestroika* are Russian words, meaning "openness" and "restructuring", which have migrated into English. Gorbachev introduced both concepts into Soviet politics and government. Glasnost was the desire to introduce openness, transparency, into government along with its gradual democratization. Perestroika was the desire, actually almost the desperate need, to restructure the failing Soviet economy and the sluggish and rigid Soviet system. Reducing rigidity would save the system, which Gorbachev still believed could be saved.

Glasnost got off to a bad start. It took Gorbachev a year to consolidate his power in the ruling Politburo by replacing and reshuffling members. Just after that, in April 1986, the accident at the Chernobyl nuclear power plant occurred, the worst nuclear accident ever. The Soviets were silent for several days while radiation spread. Their silence was very much in keeping with their standard practice. Reform efforts soon got back on track, though, with the government approval of multicandidate elections for local offices. At the same time, relations began to warm with the West, particularly with the United States and Great Britain. George H.W. Bush replaced Ronald Reagan in January 1989. He was criticized for failing to respond to the dynamic events of that year, but it can be argued that "hands-off" was the best policy.

THE FALL OF THE OUTER EMPIRE

The "outer empire" was the term used to describe the Soviet satellite states of Eastern Europe. The Iron Curtain, it can be said, was the border between the outer empire and the outside world. This was the arbitrary border, the unnatural division cutting off the natural interplay of people. Gorbachev provided the spark for the fall of the outer empire, likely without meaning to do so. He could do little more than watch. Soviet tanks did not rumble through Eastern European capitals, as they had in Budapest in 1956 and Prague in 1968. Had they done so, this probably would have destroyed peaceful reform in the Soviet Union.

Gorbachev even helped the reform process along in the outer empire. In the fall of 1988, he visited Poland. Shortly after that, Polish President Wojciech Jaruzelski proposed talks with the banned Solidarity labor movement. The June 1989 elections brought Solidarity to power in Poland. Gorbachev even persuaded the Communists to serve as minority members of the new government. In November 1989, the foreign minister of Bulgaria stopped in Moscow on his way home from China. A few days late, the long-time boss of Bulgaria, Todor Zhivkov, was ousted. In March 1989, Gorbachev went to Beijing. His visit greatly encouraged the demonstrating Chinese students. Unfortunately, April saw the Tiananmen Square crackdown, with the deaths of an estimated 3,000 demonstrators.

Romanian President Nicolae Ceausescu, long experienced in defying Moscow, tried to remain apart from the liberalizing trend. His brand of Stalin-like repression seemed likely to remain an unfortunate exception to the events of 1989. At the end of December, however, a revolt toppled him from power. Ceausescu and his wife were executed almost immediately. Their record of brutality likely would have brought them well-deserved death sentences in a trial. Some observers, however, had the feeling the two were not punished so much as silenced, to cover the involvement in Ceausescu's crimes of some of those who overthrew him.

CZECHOSLOVAKIA

Czechoslovakia was also busy that year and that December. In April 1989, in response to a question, Czech Communist Party leader Milos Jakes said he did not anticipate any present or future political role for Alexander Dubcek. After years of obscurity, Dubcek had reappeared in public to criticize the Czech government record on human rights. Jakes still thought it a safe prediction to state that Dubcek would never again have any real power or influence. No one even bothered to ask about activist playwright Vaclav Havel.

On August 21, 1989, police forcefully broke up a demonstration in Prague on the twenty-first anniversary of the Soviet invasion and the end of the Prague Spring. The police, however, were more restrained than they had been a year before at the twentieth anniversary demonstrations. In September and October, Prague became the main transit point for East German refugees fleeing to the West. In November, the government crushed further pro-democracy demonstrations.

By the end of December, however, demonstrators were again marching through the streets of Prague, singing the "Battle Hymn of the Republic" and quoting Thomas Jefferson. The Velvet Revolution was under way. The year ended with Vaclav Havel as president of Czechoslovakia. Alexander Dubcek was elected chairman of the National Assembly. Czechoslovakia has since split into the Czech Republic and Slovakia. Their revolution, though, was peaceful, and at least the former remains securely democratic.

COME TO BERLIN

Since Berlin had last been in world news, there had been some seemingly significant changes. Primarily, both West and East Germany had become accepted as legitimate governments. They even had diplomatic relations with each other. The issue of eventual reunification, however, had become a topic of world discussion, with experts confidently predicting that it would happen or that it would not happen. No one, however, anticipated how soon it would happen. Early in 1989, a leading East German Communist political theorist rejected the idea of Soviet-style democratization in East Germany. Gorbachev's primary motivation for political reforms in the Soviet Union was to rescue the economy. The East German economy seemed the strongest in the Eastern bloc. Why change? East Germans, however, looked west, a process becoming far easier. It was little consolation to the East Germans that they were better off than the Albanians when they could see how much better off people were in the West German capitalist democracy. Still, the East German government showed little inclination to liberalize.

Then came August 1989. A large group of East Germans were at a picnic in Hungary. The Hungarians had already removed the border fortifications facing Austria. They now opened the gates, and 661 East Germans celebrated European Unity Day by walking across the border into Austria. Eventually, 325,000 East Germans would join them, a far faster rate than the rate in 1961 that caused the Berlin Wall to be built. The same types of people were fleeing, too: the young and the educated. With Gorbachev's permission, the Hungarians made no effort to stop the flow.

Early in October, Gorbachev visited East Germany, to be greeted by huge, cheering crowds. A few days later, 100,000 East Germans demonstrated for democracy in Leipzig, near Berlin, the largest unauthorized demonstration in Germany since 1953. Erich Honecker, party leader since 1971, was removed from office a few days later, to be replaced by Egon Krenz. Krenz had a reputation as a hard liner when he had been head of domestic security. A few weeks earlier, however, he had persuaded Honecker to revoke an order for force against demonstrators. Showing that he was not totally realistic, in a November 1 meeting in Moscow with Gorbachev, Krenz said that demolishing the Berlin Wall was "unrealistic."[95] Somewhere between 500,000 and

On the early morning of November 11, 1989 hundreds of Berliners climbed onto the wall in the Brandenburg section of the city demanding that the wall be pulled down.

1,000,000 people demonstrated in East Berlin on November 4. In that week alone, 50,000 East Germans fled west through Czechoslovakia.

November 9, 1989, would come to be considered one of the most important days in world history. That morning, in attempting to solve the problem of refugees crowding into Prague, the government passed new regulations to permit travel but with visas. Basically, the Krenz government was opening the borders.

Crowds began to gather that evening at the wall. A photographer watching from the Western side of the wall noted, "by now the Guards didn't look aggressive and they had not a clue what was going on ... They didn't pull back behind the wall in formation. They looked very undecided among themselves. First one or two pulled back, then a few more, then a few more ...."[96]

That evening, on both sides of the wall, crowds were so great that local border commanders, unable to reach central headquarters for instructions, ordered the gates in the Berlin Wall opened. One commander told his men, "We don't need to press our rights, we need to just let this happen. This is a moment for the German people."[97]

The commander at another checkpoint, Bornholmer Strasse, was very concerned at the crowds on both sides and the potential for serious trouble. He got no help from his immediate superior. The commander told his men, "It cannot be held any longer. We have to open the checkpoint. I will discontinue the checks and let the people out."[98] When he called his wife to tell her what was happening, she at first thought he was joking.

The newsbreaks on American television that evening featured some of the most remarkable images ever seen. It was about 4 A.M. in Berlin. People were not only crossing the Berlin Wall, they were dancing on top of the symbol of the Cold War, the physical manifestation of the Iron Curtain.

POSTSCRIPT AND CONCLUSIONS

Discussing his decision to open one checkpoint, an East German border commander was told by an associate, "That's it, that's the end of the GDR."[99] The associate was right. The wall seemed not only to be holding in the people of East Germany but holding up the country. It had become more than an arbitrary border. The Berlin Wall had become a structural support. East Germany survived the fall of the Iron Curtain by just about a year. Germany was reunited on October 3, 1990.

This section of the Berlin Wall is festooned with graffiti and has been preserved as a part of history.

The Soviet Union also did not survive the end of the Iron Curtain for long. Its fall is dated to December 25, 1991, when Gorbachev suspended his functions as president. The plotters of the August 1991 coup had wanted to bring down Gorbachev. They did, but he was replaced by Boris Yeltsin, who rose to prominence to become president of Russia.

By most objective measures, the fall of the Iron Curtain and the democratization of Eastern Europe was one of the most positive developments of modern history. The countries are in different economic conditions now, with democracy functioning to different degrees. One country that straddled the Iron Curtain, Yugoslavia, at least for a while was far worse off than during the height of the Cold War.

Politically, economically, and culturally, the nations of Eastern Europe are developing naturally, without the unnatural restraints of the symbolic Iron Curtain and the real Soviet Union. Some "decadent" Western culture had always seeped through and had been considered a threat by the different regimes. It had been dangerous to deviate from approved artistic styles and standards, even if one stayed away from politics. Eastern Europeans would now have the chance to develop without the constraints of socialist conformity. They would even have the chance to judge Western culture objectively, without it having the appeal of something forbidden by disliked governments.

The West, perhaps even without meaning to, had stumbled on the right way to handle the Soviet Union and win the Cold War. Kennan had been correct in his version of containment—to resist Soviet expansion, to avoid giving them the targets of opportunity of poverty and instability, but to avoid provoking Soviet paranoia and fear of the outside world.

Inherent weaknesses in the Soviet system would cause eventual collapse. One issue raised in discussion of the Cold War and the Iron Curtain was that of how both major powers had entered World War II: by surprise attack. A basic and eminently logical foundation of national security policy in the Soviet Union and in the United States was to keep this from happening again. Ironically, for all the problems it created for the people of Europe, the arbitrary border so aptly called the Iron Curtain proved valuable in maintaining this uneasy peace. Arbitrary borders may be artificial, they may be created with little regard for the people they affect, but they have some logic behind them.

The arbitrary border of the Iron Curtain provided a security shield for the Soviets, particularly one to make them feel secure. The Iron Curtain provided a spur to Western Europe and the United States to strengthen economies and conventional defenses, to avoid offering a target of opportunity to the Soviets. For both sides, the Iron Curtain pushed back the potential time when one or the other, from design or from panic, might reach for nuclear weapons. With its negative impact on the lives of people in Eastern Europe, the Iron Curtain was an arbitrary border in all the negative senses of that term. The Iron Curtain cannot be called a good thing, but it was a useful thing.

Even something as good as the fall of the Iron Curtain was not an unmixed blessing. The Cold War had provided a discipline to world conflict with the ever-present fear that a regional conflict could grow beyond control into a major superpower confrontation. The end of the Cold War ended this restraint. Even before the Soviet Union finally collapsed, Saddam Hussein ordered the Iraqi seizure of Kuwait, leading to the 1991 Gulf War and, eventually, the 2003 Iraq War. Several conflicts occurred in Yugoslavia as that country broke up. International terrorism is a far more deadly danger now than when the Soviets were around. Even in their wildest dreams, though, Al Qaeda is not the danger the Soviets were. Despite their conservative nature, however unlikely full-scale nuclear war was between the superpowers, it could never be totally ruled out. Americans may not feel safer in this era of color-coded threat levels, but Americans are safer now than they were 20 years ago.

GEORGE KENNAN, "THE SOURCES OF SOVIET CONDUCT"

The single document that best illustrated American anti-communism and general suspicion of Soviet aspirations, was George Kennan's famous *Long Telegram* of 1946. The *Long Telegram* was perhaps the most cited and most influential statement of the early years of the Cold War.

George Kennan had been a American diplomat on the Soviet front, beginning his career as an observer of the aftermath of the Russian Civil War. He witnessed collectivization and the terror from close range and sent his telegram after another two years' service in Moscow from 1944 to 1946 as chief of mission and Ambassador Averell Harriman's consultant. In 1946, Kennan was 44 years old, fluent in the Russian language and its affairs, and decidedly anti-communist.

The essence of Kennan's telegram was published in *Foreign Affairs* in 1947 as *The Sources of Soviet Conduct* and circulated everywhere. The article was signed by "X" although everyone in the know knew that authorship was Kennan's. For Kennan, the Cold War gave the United States its historic opportunity to assume leadership of what would eventually be described as the "free world."

*   *   *   *   *

THE SOURCES OF SOVIET CONDUCT

By X

Part I

The political personality of Soviet power as we know it today is the product of ideology and circumstances: ideology inherited by the present Soviet leaders from the movement in which they had their political origin, and circumstances of the power which they now have exercised for nearly three decades in Russia. There can be few tasks of psychological analysis more difficult than to try to trace the interaction of these two forces and the relative role of each in the determination of official Soviet conduct. yet the attempt must be made if that conduct is to be understood and effectively countered.

It is difficult to summarize the set of ideological concepts with which the Soviet leaders came into power. Marxian ideology, in its Russian-

Communist projection, has always been in process of subtle evolution. The materials on which it bases itself are extensive and complex. But the outstanding features of Communist thought as it existed in 1916 may perhaps be summarized as follows: (a) that the central factor in the life of man, the factor which determines the character of public life and the "physiognomy of society," is the system by which material goods are produced and exchanged; (b) that the capitalist system of production is a nefarious one which inevitable leads to the exploitation of the working class by the capital-owning class and is incapable of developing adequately the economic resources of society or of distributing fairly the material good produced by human labor; (c) that capitalism contains the seeds of its own destruction and must, in view of the inability of the capital-owning class to adjust itself to economic change, result eventually and inescapably in a revolutionary transfer of power to the working class; and (d) that imperialism, the final phase of capitalism, leads directly to war and revolution.

The rest may be outlined in Lenin's own words: "Unevenness of economic and political development is the inflexible law of capitalism. It follows from this that the victory of Socialism may come originally in a few capitalist countries or even in a single capitalist country. The victorious proletariat of that country, having expropriated the capitalists and having organized Socialist production at home, would rise against the remaining capitalist world, drawing to itself in the process the oppressed classes of other countries." It must be noted that there was no assumption that capitalism would perish without proletarian revolution. A final push was needed from a revolutionary proletariat movement in order to tip over the tottering structure. But it was regarded as inevitable that sooner of later that push be given.

For 50 years prior to the outbreak of the Revolution, this pattern of thought had exercised great fascination for the members of the Russian revolutionary movement. Frustrated, discontented, hopeless of finding self-expression—or too impatient to seek it—in the confining limits of the Tsarist political system, yet lacking wide popular support or their choice of bloody revolution as a means of social betterment, these revolutionists found in Marxist theory a highly convenient rationalization for their own instinctive desires. It afforded pseudo-scientific justification for their impatience, for their categoric denial of all value in the Tsarist system, for their yearning for power and revenge and for their inclination to cut corners in the pursuit of it. It is therefore no wonder that they had come to believe implicitly in the truth and soundness of the Marxist-Leninist teachings, so congenial to their own impulses and emotions. Their sincerity need not be impugned. This is a phenomenon as old as human nature itself. It is has never been more aptly described than by Edward Gibbon, who wrote in *The Decline and Fall of the Roman Empire*: "From enthusiasm to imposture the step is perilous and slippery; the demon of Socrates affords a memorable instance of how a wise man may deceive himself, how a good man may deceive others, how the conscience may slumber in a mixed and middle state between self-illusion and voluntary fraud." And it was with this set of conceptions that the members of the Bolshevik Party entered into power.

Now it must be noted that through all the years of preparation for revolution, the attention of these men, as indeed of Marx himself, had been centered less on the future form which Socialism would take than on the necessary overthrow of rival power which, in their view, had to precede the introduction of Socialism. Their views, therefore, on the positive program to be put into effect, once power was attained, were for the most part nebulous, visionary and impractical. beyond the nationalization of industry and the expropriation of large private capital holdings there was no agreed program. The treatment of the peasantry, which, according to the Marxist formulation was not of the proletariat, had always been a vague spot in the pattern of Communist thought: and it remained an object of controversy and vacillation for the first ten years of Communist power.

The circumstances of the immediate post-revolution period—the existence in Russia of civil war and foreign intervention, together with the obvious fact that the Communists represented only a tiny minority of the Russian people—made the establishment of dictatorial power a necessity. The experiment with "war Communism" and the abrupt attempt to eliminate private production and trade had unfortunate economic consequences and caused further bitterness against the new revolutionary regime. While the temporary relaxation of the effort to communize Russia, represented by the New Economic Policy, alleviated some of this economic distress and thereby served its purpose, it also made it evident that the "capitalistic sector of society" was still prepared to profit at once from any relaxation of governmental pressure, and would, if permitted to continue to exist, always constitute a powerful opposing element to the Soviet regime and a serious rival for influence in the country. Somewhat the same situation prevailed with respect to the individual peasant who, in his own small way, was also a private producer.

Lenin, had he lived, might have proved a great enough man to reconcile these conflicting forces to the ultimate benefit of Russian society, thought this is questionable. But be that as it may, Stalin, and those whom he led in the struggle for succession to Lenin's position of leadership, were not the men to tolerate rival political forces in the sphere of power which they coveted. Their sense of insecurity was too great. Their particular brand of fanaticism, unmodified by any of the Anglo-Saxon traditions of compromise, was too fierce and too jealous to envisage any permanent sharing of power. From the Russian-Asiatic world out of which they had emerged they carried with them a skepticism as to the possibilities of permanent and peaceful coexistence of rival forces. Easily persuaded of their own doctrinaire "rightness," they insisted on the submission or destruction of all competing power. Outside the Communist Party, Russian society was to have no rigidity. There were to be no forms of collective human activity or association which would not be dominated by the Party. No other force in Russian society was to be permitted to achieve vitality or integrity. Only the Party was to have structure. All else was to be an amorphous mass.

And within the Party the same principle was to apply. The mass of Party members might go through the motions of election, deliberation, decision and action; but in these motions they were to be animated not by their own individual wills but by the awesome breath of the Party leadership and the overbrooding presence of "the word."

Let it be stressed again that subjectively these men probably did not seek absolutism for its own sake. They doubtless believed—and found it easy to believe—that they alone knew what was good for society and that they would accomplish that good once their power was secure and unchallengeable. But in seeking that security of their own rule they were prepared to recognize no restrictions, either of God or man, on

123

the character of their methods. And until such time as that security might be achieved, they placed far down on their scale of operational priorities the comforts and happiness of the peoples entrusted to their care.

Now the outstanding circumstance concerning the Soviet regime is that down to the present day this process of political consolidation has never been completed and the men in the Kremlin have continued to be predominantly absorbed with the struggle to secure and make absolute the power which they seized in November 1917. They have endeavored to secure it primarily against forces at home, within Soviet society itself. But they have also endeavored to secure it against the outside world. For ideology, as we have seen, taught them that the outside world was hostile and that it was their duty eventually to overthrow the political forces beyond their borders. Then powerful hands of Russian history and tradition reached up to sustain them in this feeling. Finally, their own aggressive intransigence with respect to the outside world began to find its own reaction; and they were soon forced, to use another Gibbonesque phrase, "to chastise the contumacy" which they themselves had provoked. It is an undeniable privilege of every man to prove himself right in the thesis that the world is his enemy; for if he reiterates it frequently enough and makes it the background of his conduct he is bound eventually to be right.

Now it lies in the nature of the mental world of the Soviet leaders, as well as in the character of their ideology, that no opposition to them can be officially recognized as having any merit or justification whatsoever. Such opposition can flow, in theory, only from the hostile and incorrigible forces of dying capitalism. As long as remnants of capitalism were officially recognized as existing in Russia, it was possible to place on them, as an internal element, part of the blame for the maintenance of a dictatorial form of society. But as these remnants were liquidated, little by little, this justification fell away, and when it was indicated officially that they had been finally destroyed, it disappeared altogether. And this fact created one of the most basic of the compulsions which came to act upon the Soviet regime: since capitalism no longer existed in Russia and since it could not be admitted that there could be serious or widespread opposition to the Kremlin springing spontaneously from the liberated masses under its authority, it became necessary to justify the retention of the dictatorship by stressing the menace of capitalism abroad.

This began at an early date. In 1924 Stalin specifically defended the retention of the "organs of suppression," meaning, among others, the army and the secret police, on the ground that "as long as there is a capitalistic encirclement there will be danger of intervention with all the consequences that flow from that danger." In accordance with that theory, and from that time on, all internal opposition forces in Russia have consistently been portrayed as the agents of foreign forces of reaction antagonistic to Soviet power.

By the same token, tremendous emphasis has been placed on the original Communist thesis of a basic antagonism between the capitalist and Socialist worlds. It is clear, from many indications, that this emphasis is not founded in reality. The real facts concerning it have been confused by the existence abroad of genuine resentment provoked by Soviet philosophy and tactics and occasionally by the existence of great centers of military power, notably the Nazi regime in Germany and the Japanese Government of the late 1930s, which indeed have aggressive designs against the Soviet Union. But there is ample evidence that the stress laid in Moscow on the menace confronting Soviet society from the world outside its borders is founded not in the realities of foreign antagonism but in the necessity of explaining away the maintenance of dictatorial authority at home.

Now the maintenance of this pattern of Soviet power, namely, the pursuit of unlimited authority domestically, accompanied by the cultivation of the semi-myth of implacable foreign hostility, has gone far to shape the actual machinery of Soviet power as we know it today. Internal organs of administration which did not serve this purpose withered on the vine. Organs which did serve this purpose became vastly swollen. The security of Soviet power came to rest on the iron discipline of the Party, on the severity and ubiquity of the secret police, and on the uncompromising economic monopolism of the state. The "organs of suppression," in which the Soviet leaders had sought security from rival forces, became in large measures the masters of those whom they were designed to serve. Today the major part of the structure of Soviet power is committed to the perfection of the dictatorship and to the maintenance of the concept of Russia as in a state of siege, with the enemy lowering beyond the walls. And the millions of human beings who form that part of the structure of power must defend at all costs this concept of Russia's position, for without it they are themselves superfluous.

As things stand today, the rulers can no longer dream of parting with these organs of suppression. The quest for absolute power, pursued now for nearly three decades with a ruthlessness unparalleled (in scope at least) in modern times, has again produced internally, as it did externally, its own reaction. The excesses of the police apparatus have fanned the potential opposition to the regime into something far greater and more dangerous than it could have been before those excesses began.

But least of all can the rulers dispense with the fiction by which the maintenance of dictatorial power has been defended. For this fiction has been canonized in Soviet philosophy by the excesses already committed in its name; and it is now anchored in the Soviet structure of thought by bonds far greater than those of mere ideology.

Part II

So much for the historical background. What does it spell in terms of the political personality of Soviet power as we know it today?

Of the original ideology, nothing has been officially junked. Belief is maintained in the basic badness of capitalism, in the inevitability of its destruction, in the obligation of the proletariat to assist in that destruction and to take power into its own hands. But stress has come to be laid primarily on those concepts which relate most specifically to the Soviet regime itself: to its position as the sole truly Socialist regime in a dark and misguided world, and to the relationships of power within it.

The first of these concepts is that of the innate antagonism between capitalism and Socialism. We have seen how deeply that concept has become imbedded in foundations of Soviet power. It has profound implications for Russia's conduct as a member of international society. It means that there can never be on Moscow's side an sincere assumption of a community of aims between the Soviet Union and powers which are regarded as capitalist. It must inevitably be assumed in Moscow that the aims of the capitalist world are antagonistic to the Soviet regime, and therefore to the interests of the peoples it controls. If the Soviet government occasionally sets it signature to documents which would indicate the contrary, this is to regarded as a tactical maneuver permissible in dealing with the enemy (who is without honor) and should be taken in the spirit of *caveat emptor*. Basically, the antagonism remains. It is postulated. And from it flow many of the phenomena which we find disturbing in the Kremlin's conduct of foreign policy: the secretiveness, the lack of frankness, the duplicity, the wary suspiciousness, and the basic unfriendliness of purpose. These phenomena are there to stay, for the foreseeable future. There can be variations of degree and of emphasis. When there is something the Russians want from us, one or the other of these features of their policy may be thrust temporarily into the background; and when that happens there will always be Americans who will leap forward with gleeful announcements that "the Russians have changed," and some who will even try to take credit for having brought about such "changes." But we should not be misled by tactical maneuvers. These characteristics of Soviet policy, like the postulate from which they flow, are basic to the internal nature of Soviet power, and will be with us, whether in the foreground or the background, until the internal nature of Soviet power is changed.

This means we are going to continue for long time to find the Russians difficult to deal with. It does not mean that they should be considered as embarked upon a do-or-die program to overthrow our society by a given date. The theory of the inevitability of the eventual fall of capitalism has the fortunate connotation that there is no hurry about it. The forces of progress can take their time in preparing the final *coup de grâce*. meanwhile, what is vital is that the "Socialist fatherland"—that oasis of power which has already been won for Socialism in the person of the Soviet Union—should be cherished and defended by all good Communists at home and abroad, its fortunes promoted, its enemies badgered and confounded. The promotion of premature, "adventuristic" revolutionary projects abroad which might embarrass Soviet power in any way would be an inexcusable, even a counter-revolutionary act. The cause of Socialism is the support and promotion of Soviet power, as defined in Moscow.

This brings us to the second of the concepts important to contemporary Soviet outlook. That is the infallibility of the Kremlin. The Soviet concept of power, which permits no focal points of organization outside the Party itself, requires that the Party leadership remain in theory the sole repository of truth. For if truth were to be found elsewhere, there would be justification for its expression in organized activity. But it is precisely that which the Kremlin cannot and will not permit.

The leadership of the Communist Party is therefore always right, and has been always right ever since in 1929 Stalin formalized his personal power by announcing that decisions of the Politburo were being taken unanimously.

On the principle of infallibility there rests the iron discipline of the Communist Party. In fact, the two concepts are mutually self-supporting. Perfect discipline requires recognition of infallibility. Infallibility requires the observance of discipline. And the two go far to determine the behaviorism of the entire Soviet apparatus of power. But their effect cannot be understood unless a third factor be taken into account: namely, the fact that the leadership is at liberty to put forward for tactical purposes any particular thesis which it finds useful to the cause at any particular moment and to require the faithful and unquestioning acceptance of that thesis by the members of the movement as a whole. This means that truth is not a constant but is actually created, for all intents and purposes, by the Soviet leaders themselves. It may vary from week to week, from month to month. It is nothing absolute and immutable—nothing which flows from objective reality. It is only the most recent manifestation of the wisdom of those in whom the ultimate wisdom is supposed to reside, because they represent the logic of history. The accumulative effect of these factors is to give to the whole subordinate apparatus of Soviet power an unshakable stubbornness and steadfastness in its orientation. This orientation can be changed at will by the Kremlin but by no other power. Once a given party line has been laid down on a given issue of current policy, the whole Soviet governmental machine, including the mechanism of diplomacy, moves inexorably along the prescribed path, like a persistent toy automobile wound up and headed in a given direction, stopping only when it meets with some unanswerable force. The individuals who are the components of this machine are unamenable to argument or reason, which comes to them from outside sources. Their whole training has taught them to mistrust and discount the glib persuasiveness of the outside world. Like the white dog before the phonograph, they hear only the "master's voice." And if they are to be called off from the purposes last dictated to them, it is the master who must call them off. Thus the foreign representative cannot hope that his words will make any impression on them. The most that he can hope is that they will be transmitted to those at the top, who are capable of changing the party line. But even those are not likely to be swayed by any normal logic in the words of the bourgeois representative. Since there can be no appeal to common purposes, there can be no appeal to common mental approaches. For this reason, facts speak louder than words to the ears of the Kremlin; and words carry the greatest weight when they have the ring of reflecting, or being backed up by, facts of unchallengeable validity.

But we have seen that the Kremlin is under no ideological compulsion to accomplish its purposes in a hurry. Like the Church, it is dealing in ideological concepts which are of long-term validity, and it can afford to be patient. It has no right to risk the existing achievements of the revolution for the sake of vain baubles of the future. The very teachings of Lenin himself require great caution and flexibility in the pursuit of Communist purposes. Again, these precepts are fortified by the lessons of Russian history: of centuries of obscure battles between nomadic forces over the stretches of a vast unfortified plain. Here caution, circumspection, flexibility and deception are the valuable qualities; and their value finds a natural appreciation in the Russian or the oriental mind. Thus the Kremlin has no compunction about retreating in the face of superior forces. And being under the compulsion of no timetable, it does not get panicky under the necessity for such retreat. Its political action is a fluid stream which moves constantly, wherever it is permitted to move, toward a given goal. Its main concern is to make sure that it has filled every nook and cranny available to it in the basin of world power. But if it finds unassailable barriers in its path, it accepts these philosophically and accommodates itself to them. The main thing is that there should always be pressure, unceasing constant pressure, toward the desired goal. There is no trace of any feeling in Soviet psychology that that goal must be reached at any given time.

These considerations make Soviet diplomacy at once easier and more difficult to deal with than the diplomacy of individual aggressive leaders like Napoleon and Hitler. On the one hand it is more sensitive to contrary force, more ready to yield on individual sectors of the diplomatic front when that force is felt to be too strong, and thus more rational in the logic and rhetoric of power. On the other hand it cannot be easily defeated or discouraged by a single victory on the part of its opponents. And the patient persistence by which it is animated means that it can be effectively countered not by sporadic acts which represent the momentary whims of democratic opinion but only be intelligent long-range policies on the part of Russia's adversaries—policies no less steady in their purpose, and no less variegated and resourceful in their application, than those of the Soviet Union itself.

In these circumstances it is clear that the main element of any United States policy toward the Soviet Union must be that of long-term, patient but firm and vigilant containment of Russian expansive tendencies. It is important to note, however, that such a policy has nothing to do with outward histrionics: with threats or blustering or superfluous gestures of outward "toughness." While the Kremlin is basically flexible in its reaction to political realities, it is by no means unamenable to considerations of prestige. Like almost any other government, it can be placed by tactless and threatening gestures in a position where it cannot afford to yield even though this might be dictated by its sense of realism. The Russian leaders are keen judges of human psychology, and as such they are highly conscious that loss of temper and of self-control is never a source of strength in political affairs. They are quick to exploit such evidences of weakness. For these reasons it is a *sine qua non* of successful dealing with Russia that the foreign government in question should remain at all times cool and collected and that its demands on Russian policy should be put forward in such a manner as to leave the way open for a compliance not too detrimental to Russian prestige.

Part III

In the light of the above, it will be clearly seen that the Soviet pressure against the free institutions of the western world is something that can be contained by the adroit and vigilant application of counter-force at a series of constantly shifting geographical and political points, corresponding to the shifts and maneuvers of Soviet policy, but which cannot be charmed or talked out of existence. The Russians look forward to a duel of infinite duration, and they see that already they have scored great successes. It must be borne in mind that there was a time when the Communist Party represented far more of a minority in the sphere of Russian national life than Soviet power today represents in the world community.

But if the ideology convinces the rulers of Russia that truth is on their side and they they can therefore afford to wait, those of us on whom that ideology has no claim are free to examine objectively the validity of that premise. The Soviet thesis not only implies complete lack of control by the west over its own economic destiny, it likewise assumes Russian unity, discipline and patience over an infinite period. Let us bring this apocalyptic vision down to earth, and suppose that the western world finds the strength and resourcefulness to contain Soviet power over a period of ten to fifteen years. What does that spell for Russia itself?

The Soviet leaders, taking advantage of the contributions of modern techniques to the arts of despotism, have solved the question of obedience within the confines of their power. Few challenge their authority; and even those who do are unable to make that challenge valid as against the organs of suppression of the state.

The Kremlin has also proved able to accomplish its purpose of building up Russia, regardless of the interests of the inhabitants, and industrial foundation of heavy metallurgy, which is, to be sure, not yet complete but which is nevertheless continuing to grow and is approaching those of the other major industrial countries. All of this, however, both the maintenance of internal political security and the building of heavy industry, has been carried out at a terrible cost in human life and in human hopes and energies. It has necessitated the use of forced labor on a scale unprecedented in modern times under conditions of peace. It has involved the neglect or abuse of other phases of Soviet economic life, particularly agriculture, consumers' goods production, housing and transportation.

To all that, the war has added its tremendous toll of destruction, death and human exhaustion. In consequence of this, we have in Russia today a population which is physically and spiritually tired. The mass of the people are disillusioned, skeptical and no longer as accessible as they once were to the magical attraction which Soviet power still radiates to its followers abroad. The avidity with which people seized upon the slight respite accorded to the Church for tactical reasons during the war was eloquent testimony to the fact that their capacity for faith and devotion found little expression in the purposes of the regime.

In these circumstances, there are limits to the physical and nervous strength of people themselves. These limits are absolute ones, and are binding even for the cruelest dictatorship, because beyond them people cannot be driven. The forced labor camps and the other agencies of constraint provide temporary means of compelling people to work longer hours than their own volition or mere economic pressure would dictate; but if people survive them at all they become old before their time and must be considered as human casualties to the demands of dictatorship. In either case their best powers are no longer available to society and can no longer be enlisted in the service of the state.

Here only the younger generations can help. The younger generation, despite all vicissitudes and sufferings, is numerous and vigorous; and the Russians are a talented people. But it still remains to be seen what will be the effects on mature performance of the abnormal emotional strains of childhood which Soviet dictatorship created and which were enormously increased by the war. Such things as normal security and placidity of home environment have practically ceased to exist in the Soviet Union outside of the most remote farms and villages. And observers are not yet sure whether that is not going to leave its mark on the over-all capacity of the generation now coming into maturity.

In addition to this, we have the fact that Soviet economic development, while it can list certain formidable achievements, has been precariously spotty and uneven. Russian Communists who speak of the "uneven development of capitalism" should blush at the contemplation of their own national economy. Here certain branches of economic life, such as the metallurgical and machine industries, have been pushed out of all proportion to other sectors of economy. Here is a nation striving to become in a short period one of the great industrial nations of the world while it still has no highway network worthy of the name and only a relatively primitive network of railways. Much has been done to increase efficiency of labor and to teach primitive peasants something about the operation of machines. But maintenance is still a crying deficiency of all Soviet economy. Construction is hasty and poor in quality. Depreciation must be enormous. And in vast sectors of economic life it has not yet been possible to instill into labor anything like that general culture of production and technical self-respect which characterizes the skilled worker of the west.

It is difficult to see how these deficiencies can be corrected at an early date by a tired and dispirited population working largely under the shadow of fear and compulsion. And as long as they are not overcome, Russia will remain economically as vulnerable, and in a certain sense an impotent, nation, capable of exporting its enthusiasms and of radiating the strange charm of its primitive political vitality but unable to back up those articles of export by the real evidences of material power and prosperity.

Meanwhile, a great uncertainty hangs over the political life of the Soviet Union. That is the uncertainty involved in the transfer of power from one individual or group of individuals to others.

This is, of course, outstandingly the problem of the personal position of Stalin. We must remember that his succession to Lenin's pinnacle of pre-eminence in the Communist movement was the only such transfer of individual authority which the Soviet Union has experienced. That transfer took 12 years to consolidate. It cost the lives of millions of people and shook the state to its foundations. The attendant tremors were felt all through the international revolutionary movement, to the disadvantage of the Kremlin itself.

It is always possible that another transfer of pre-eminent power may take place quietly and inconspicuously, with no repercussions anywhere. But again, it is possible that the questions involved may unleash, to use some of Lenin's words, one of those "incredibly swift transitions" from "delicate deceit" to "wild violence" which characterize Russian history, and may shake Soviet power to its foundations.

But this is not only a question of Stalin himself. There has been, since 1938, a dangerous congealment of political life in the higher circles of Soviet power. The All-Union Congress of Soviets, in theory the supreme body of the Party, is supposed to meet not less often than once in three years. It will soon be eight full years since its last meeting. During this period membership in the Party has numerically doubled. Party mortality during the war was enormous; and today well over half of the Party members are persons who have entered since the last Party congress was held. meanwhile, the same small group of men has carried on at the top through an amazing series of national vicissitudes. Surely there is some reason why the experiences of the war brought basic political changes to every one of the great governments of the west. Surely the causes of that phenomenon are basic enough to be present somewhere in the obscurity of Soviet political life, as well. And yet no recognition has been given to these causes in Russia.

It must be surmised from this that even within so highly disciplined an organization as the Communist Party there must be a growing divergence in age, outlook and interest between the great mass of Party members, only so recently recruited into the movement, and the little self-perpetuating clique of men at the top, whom most of these Party members have never met, with whom they have never conversed, and with whom they can have no political intimacy.

Who can say whether, in these circumstances, the eventual rejuvenation of the higher spheres of authority (which can only be a matter of time) can take place smoothly and peacefully, or whether rivals in the quest for higher power will not eventually reach down into these politically immature and inexperienced masses in order to find support for their respective claims? If this were ever to happen, strange consequences could flow for the Communist Party: for the membership at large has been exercised only in the practices of iron discipline and obedience and not in the arts of compromise and accommodation. And if disunity were ever to seize and paralyze the Party, the chaos and weakness of Russian society would be revealed in forms beyond description. For we have seen that Soviet power is only concealing an amorphous mass of human beings among whom no independent organizational structure is tolerated. In Russia there is not even such a thing as local government. The present generation of Russians have never known spontaneity of collective action. If, consequently, anything were ever to occur to disrupt the unity and efficacy of the Party as a political instrument, Soviet Russia might be changed overnight from one of the strongest to one of the weakest and most pitiable of national societies.

Thus the future of Soviet power may not be by any means as secure as Russian capacity for self-delusion would make it appear to the men of the

Kremlin. That they can quietly and easily turn it over to others remains to be proved. Meanwhile, the hardships of their rule and the vicissitudes of international life have taken a heavy toll of the strength and hopes of the great people on whom their power rests. It is curious to note that the ideological power of Soviet authority is strongest today in areas beyond the frontiers of Russia, beyond the reach of its police power. This phenomenon brings to mind a comparison used by Thomas Mann in his great novel *Buddenbrooks.* Observing that human institutions often show the greatest outward brilliance at a moment when inner decay is in reality farthest advanced, he compared one of those stars whose light shines most brightly on this world when in reality it has long since ceased to exist. And who can say with assurance that the strong light still cast by the Kremlin on the dissatisfied peoples of the western world is not the powerful afterglow of a constellation which is in actuality on the wane? This cannot be proved. And it cannot be disproved. But the possibility remains (and in the opinion of this writer it is a strong one) that Soviet power, like the capitalist world of its conception, bears within it the seeds of its own decay, and that the sprouting of these seeds is well advanced.

Part IV

It is clear that the United States cannot expect in the foreseeable future to enjoy political intimacy with the Soviet regime. It must continue to regard the Soviet Union as a rival, not a partner, in the political arena. It must continue to expect that Soviet policies will reflect no abstract love of peace and stability, no real faith in the possibility of a permanent happy coexistence of the Socialist and capitalist worlds, but rather a cautious, persistent pressure toward the disruption and, weakening of all rival influence and rival power.

Balanced against this are the facts that Russia, as opposed to the western world in general, is still by far the weaker party, that Soviet policy is highly flexible, and that Soviet society may well contain deficiencies which will eventually weaken its own total potential. This would of itself warrant the United States entering with reasonable confidence upon a policy of firm containment, designed to confront the Russians with unalterable counter-force at every point where they show signs of encroaching upon the interests of a peaceful and stable world.

But in actuality the possibilities for American policy are by no means limited to holding the line and hoping for the best. It is entirely possible for the United States to influence by its actions the internal developments, both within Russia and throughout the international Communist movement, by which Russian policy is largely determined. This is not only a question of the modest measure of informational activity which this government can conduct in the Soviet Union and elsewhere, although that, too, is important. It is rather a question of the degree to which the United States can create among the peoples of the world generally the impression of a country which knows what it wants, which is coping successfully with the problem of its internal life and with the responsibilities of a World Power, and which has a spiritual vitality capable of holding its own among the major ideological currents of the time. To the extent that such an impression can be created and maintained, the aims of Russian Communism must appear sterile and quixotic, the hopes and enthusiasm of Moscow's supporters must wane, and added strain must be imposed on the Kremlin's foreign policies. For the palsied decrepitude of the capitalist world is the keystone of Communist philosophy. Even the failure of the United States to experience the early economic depression which the ravens of the Red Square have been predicting with such complacent confidence since hostilities ceased would have deep and important repercussions throughout the Communist world.

By the same token, exhibitions of indecision, disunity and internal disintegration within this country have an exhilarating effect on the whole Communist movement. At each evidence of these tendencies, a thrill of hope and excitement goes through the Communist world; a new jauntiness can be noted in the Moscow tread; new groups of foreign supporters climb on to what they can only view as the band wagon of international politics; and Russian pressure increases all along the line in international affairs.

It would be an exaggeration to say that American behavior unassisted and alone could exercise a power of life and death over the Communist movement and bring about the early fall of Soviet power in Russia. But the United States has it in its power to increase enormously the strains under which Soviet policy must operate, to force upon the Kremlin a far greater degree of moderation and circumspection than it has had to observe in recent years, and in this way to promote tendencies which must eventually find their outlet in either the breakup or the gradual mellowing of Soviet power. For no mystical, Messianic movement—and particularly not that of the Kremlin—can face frustration indefinitely without eventually adjusting itself in one way or another to the logic of that state of affairs.

Thus the decision will really fall in large measure in this country itself. The issue of Soviet-American relations is in essence a test of the overall worth of the United States as a nation among nations. To avoid destruction the United States need only measure up to its own best traditions and prove itself worthy of preservation as a great nation.

Surely, there was never a fairer test of national quality than this. In the light of these circumstances, the thoughtful observer of Russian-American relations will find no cause for complaint in the Kremlin's challenge to American society. He will rather experience a certain gratitude to a Providence which, by providing the American people with this implacable challenge, has made their entire security as a nation dependent on their pulling themselves together and accepting the responsibilities of moral and political leadership that history plainly intended them to bear.

Winston Churchill, The Sinews of Peace

I am glad to come to Westminster College this afternoon, and am complimented that you should give me a degree. The name "Westminster" is somehow familiar to me. I seem to have heard of it before. Indeed, it was at Westminster that I received a very large part of my education in politics, dialectic, rhetoric, and one or two other things. In fact we have both been educated at the same, or similar, or, at any rate, kindred establishments.

The United States stands at this time at the pinnacle of world power. It is a solemn moment for the American Democracy. For with primacy in power is also joined an awe-inspiring accountability to the future. If you look around you, you must feel not only the sense of duty done but also you must feel anxiety lest you fall below the level of achievement. Opportunity is here now, clear and shining for both our countries. To reject it or ignore it or fritter it away will bring upon us all the long reproaches of the after-time. It is necessary that constancy of mind, persistency of purpose, and the grand simplicity of decision shall guide and rule the conduct of the English-speaking peoples in peace as they did in war. We must, and I believe we shall, prove ourselves equal to this severe requirement.

I have a definite and practical proposal to make for action. (courts and magistrates may be set up but they cannot function without sheriffs and constables. The United Nations Organization must immediately begin to be equipped with an international armed force. In such a matter we can only go step by step, but we must begin now. I propose that each of the Powers and States should be invited to delegate a certain number of air squadrons to the service of the world organization. These squadrons would be trained and prepared in their own countries, but would move around in rotation from one country to another. They would wear the uniform of their own countries but with different badges. They would not be required to act against their own nation, but in other respects they would be directed by the world organization. This might be started on a modest scale and would grow as confidence grew. I wished to see this done after the first world war, and I devoutly trust it may be done forthwith.

It would nevertheless be wrong and imprudent to entrust the secret knowledge or experience of the atomic bomb, which the United States,

Great Britain, and Canada now share, to the world organization, while it is still in its infancy. It would be criminal madness to cast it adrift in this still agitated and un-united world. No one in any country has slept less well in their beds because this knowledge and the method and the raw materials to apply it, are at present largely retained in American hands. I do not believe we should all have slept so soundly had the positions been reversed and if some Communist or neo-Fascist State monopolized for the time being these dread agencies. The fear of them alone might easily have been used to enforce totalitarian systems upon the free democratic world, with consequences appalling to human imagination. God has willed that this shall not be and we have at least a breathing space to set our house in order before this peril has to be encountered: and even then, if no effort is spared, we should still possess so formidable a superiority as to impose effective deterrents upon its employment, or threat of employment, by others. [Ultimately, when the essential brotherhood of man is truly embodied and expressed in a world organization with all the necessary practical safeguards to make it effective, these powers would naturally be confided to that world organization.]

Now I come to the second danger of these two marauders which threaten the cottage, the home, and the ordinary people—namely, tyranny. We cannot be blind to the fact that the liberties enjoyed by individual citizens throughout the British Empire are not valid in a considerable number of countries, some of which are very powerful. In these States control is enforced upon the common people by various kinds of all-embracing police governments. The power of the State is exercised without restraint, either by dictators or by compact oligarchies operating through a privileged party and a political police. It is not our duty at this time, when difficulties are so numerous, to interfere forcibly in the internal affairs of countries which we have not conquered in war. But we must never cease to proclaim in fearless tones the great principles of freedom and the rights of man which are the joint inheritance of the English-speaking world and which through Magna Carta, the Bill of Rights, the Habeas Corpus, trial by jury, and the English common law find their most famous expression in the American Declaration of Independence.

All this means that the people of any country have the right, and should have the power by constitutional action, by free unfettered elections, with secret ballot, to choose or change the character or form of government under which they dwell; that freedom of speech and thought should reign; that courts of justice, independent of the executive, unbiased by any party, should administer laws which have received the broad assent of large majorities or are consecrated by time and custom. Here are the title deeds of freedom which should lie in every cottage home. Here is the message of the British and American peoples to mankind. Let us preach what we practice—let us practice what we preach. Neither the sure prevention of war, nor the continuous rise of world organization will be gained without what I have called the fraternal association of the English-speaking peoples. This means a special relationship between the British Commonwealth and Empire and the United States. Fraternal association requires not only the growing friendship and mutual understanding between our two vast but kindred systems of society, but the continuance of the intimate relationship between our military advisers, leading to common study of potential dangers, the similarity of weapons and manuals of instructions, and to the interchange of officers and cadets at technical colleges. It should carry with it the continuance of the present facilities for mutual security by the joint use of all Naval and Air Force bases in the possession of either country all over the world.

A shadow has fallen upon the scenes so lately lighted by the Allied victory. Nobody knows what Soviet Russia and its Communist international organization intends to do in the immediate future, or what are the limits, if any, to their expansive and proselytizing tendencies. I have a strong admiration and regard for the valiant Russian people and for my wartime comrade, Marshal Stalin. There is deep sympathy and goodwill in Britain—and I doubt not here also towards the peoples of all the Russians and a resolve to persevere through many differences and rebuffs in establishing lasting friendships. We understand the Russian need to be secure on her western frontiers by the removal of all possibility of German aggression. We welcome Russia to her rightful place among the leading nations of the world. We welcome her flag upon the seas. Above all, we welcome constant, frequent and growing contacts between the Russian people and our own people on both sides of the Atlantic. It is my duty however, for I am sure you would wish me to state the facts as I see them to you, to place before you certain facts about the present position in Europe.

From Stettin in the Baltic to Trieste in the Adriatic, an iron curtain has descended across the Continent. Behind that line lie all the capitals of the ancient states of Central and Eastern Europe. Warsaw, Berlin, Prague, Vienna, Budapest, Belgrade, Bucharest and Sofia, all these famous cities and the populations around them lie in what I must call the Soviet sphere, and all are subject in one form or another, not only to Soviet influence but to a very high and, in many cases, increasing measure of control from Moscow. Athens alone—Greece with its immortal glories— is free to decide its future at an election under British, American and French observation. The Russian-dominated Polish Government has been encouraged to make enormous and wrongful inroads upon Germany, and mass expulsions of millions of Germans on a scale griev- ous and undreamed-of are now taking place. The Communist parties, which were very small in all these Eastern States of Europe, have been raised to preeminence and power far beyond their numbers and are seek- ing everywhere to obtain totalitarian control. Police governments are prevailing in nearly every case, and so far, except in Czechoslovakia, there is no true democracy.

The safety of the world requires a new unity in Europe, from which no nation should be permanently outcast. It is from the quarrels of the strong parent races in Europe that the world wars we have witnessed, or which occurred in former times, have sprung. Twice in our own lifetime we have seen the United States, against their wishes and their traditions, against arguments, the force of which it is impossible not to comprehend, drawn by irresistible forces alto these wars in time to secure the victory of the good cause, but only after frightful slaughter and devastation had occurred. Twice the United States has had to send several millions of its young men across the Atlantic to find the war; but now war can find any nation, wherever it may dwell between dusk and dawn. Surely we should work with conscious purpose for a grand pacification of Europe, within the structure of the United Nations and in accordance with its Charter. That I feel is an open cause of policy of very great importance.

In front of the iron curtain which lies across Europe are other causes for anxiety. In Italy the Communist Party is seriously hampered by hav- ing to support the Communist-trained Marshal Tito's claims to former Italian territory at the head of the Adriatic. Nevertheless the future of

Italy hangs in the balance. Again one cannot imagine a regenerated Europe without a strong France. All my public life I have worked for a strong France and I never lost faith in her destiny, even in the darkest hours. I will not lose faith now. However, in a great number of countries, far from the Russian frontiers and throughout the world, Communist fifth columns are established and work in complete unity and absolute obedience to the directions they receive from the communist center. Except in the British Commonwealth and in the United States where Communism is in its infancy, the Communist parties or fifth columns constitute a growing challenge and peril to Christian civilization. These are somber facts for anyone to have to recite on the morrow of a victory gained by so much splendid comradeship in arms and in the cause of freedom and democracy; but we should be most unwise not to face them squarely while time remains.

I have felt bound to portray the shadow which, alike in the west and in the east, falls upon the world. I was a high minister at the time of the Versailles Treaty and a close friend of Mr. Lloyd-George, who was the head of the British delegation at Versailles. I did not myself agree with many things that were done, but I have a very strong impression in my mind of that situation, and I find it painful to contrast it with that which prevails now. In those days there were high hopes and unbounded confidence that the wars were over, and that the League of Nations would become all-powerful. I do not see or feel that same confidence or even the same hopes in the haggard world at the present time.

On the other hand I repulse the idea that a new war is inevitable; still more that it is imminent. It is because I am sure that our fortunes are still in our own hands and that we hold the power to save the future, that I feel the duty to speak out now that I have the occasion and the opportunity to do so. I do not believe that Soviet Russia desires war. What they desire is the fruits of war and the indefinite expansion of their power and doctrines. But what we have to consider here today while time remains, is the permanent prevention of war and the establishment of conditions of freedom and democracy as rapidly as possible in all countries. Our difficulties and dangers will not be removed by closing our eyes to them. They will not be removed by mere waiting to see what happens; nor will they be removed by a policy of appeasement. What is needed is a settlement, and the longer this is delayed, the more difficult it will be and the greater our dangers will become.

From what I have seen of our Russian friends and Allies during the war, I am convinced that there is nothing they admire so much as strength, and there is nothing for which they have less respect than for weakness, especially military weakness. For that reason the old doctrine of a balance of power is unsound. We cannot afford, if we can help it, to work on narrow margins, offering temptations to a trial of strength. If the Western Democracies stand together in strict adherence to the principles of the United Nations Charter, their influence for furthering those principles will be immense and no one is likely to molest them. If however they become divided or falter in their duty and if these all-important years are allowed to slip away, then indeed catastrophe may overwhelm us all.

Last time I saw it all coming and cried aloud to my own fellow-countrymen and to the world, but no one paid any attention. Up till the year 1933 or even 1935, Germany might have been saved from the awful fate which has overtaken her and we might all have been spared the miseries Hitler let loose upon mankind. There never was a war in all history easier to prevent by timely action than the one which has just desolated such great areas of the globe. It could have been prevented in my belief without the firing of a single shot, and Germany might be powerful, prosperous and honored today; but no one would listen and one by one we were all sucked into the awful whirlpool. We surely must not let that happen again. This can only be achieved by reaching now, in 1946, a good understanding on all points with Russia under the general authority of the United Nations Organization and by the maintenance of that good understanding through many peaceful years, by the world instrument, supported by the whole strength of the English-speaking world and all its connections. There is the solution which I respectfully offer to you in this Address to which I have given the title "The Sinews of Peace."

1939	September 1	Germany invades Poland.
1941	June 22	Germany invades Soviet Union.
	December 7	Japanese attack Pearl Harbor. United States enters World War II.
1945	February 4–11	Yalta Conference takes place.
1945	April 12	Harry Truman becomes president of United States.
	May 8	Germany surrenders.
	August 6	Atomic bomb is dropped over Hiroshima, Japan.
	August 15	Japan surrenders.
1946	March 5	Winston Churchill makes "Iron Curtain" speech.
1947	March 12	"Truman Doctrine" is announced.
1948	February 27	Communists take over Czechoslovakia.
	June 24	Berlin blockade starts.
1949	January 20	Truman is inaugurated to full term as resident of the United States.

February 4-11, 1945
Yalta Conference

May 8, 1945
Germany Surrenders

June 24, 1948
Berlin Blockade starts
(ends April 4, 1949)

October 29, 1956
Israel invades Sinai
Desert of Egypt

November 4, 1956
Soviet army moves
into Budapest

1945   **1955**

April 4, 1949
NATO treaty signed

March 5, 1953
Joseph Stalin dies

March 5, 1946
Winston Churchill makes
"Iron Curtain" Speech

May 14, 1954
Warsaw Pact
formed

	April 4	NATO Treaty is signed.
	May 12	Berlin blockade officially ends.
	September 23	United States announces evidence that Soviets tested atomic bomb.
	October 1	People's Republic of China is proclaimed.
1950	June 25	Korean War starts.
1953	January 20	Dwight D. Eisenhower is inaugurated as president of the United States.
	March 5	Joseph Stalin dies.
	July 27	Korean War armistice is signed.
1954	May 7	French surrender at Dien Bien Phu, Vietnam.
	July 21	Geneva Accords partition Vietnam at 17th parallel.
	December 2	Senator Joseph McCarthy is condemned by U.S. Senate.
1955	May 8	West Germany joins NATO.

December 27, 1979
Soviets invade
Afghanistan

March 11, 1985
Mikhail Gorbachev
becomes head of
Communist Party

August 19, 1961
Berlin Wall built

1960   1990

June 16, 1963
Kennedy delivers
his "Ich bin ein
Berliner" speech

November 9, 1989
Berlin Wall falls

August 21, 1968
Soviet and Warsaw
Pact troops occupy
Prague to crush reforms

	May 14	Warsaw Pact is formed.
1956	July 26	Gamel Nasser nationalizes Suez Canal.
	October 29	Israel invades Sinai Desert of Egypt.
	November 1	Nagy government in Hungary announces withdrawal from Warsaw Pact.
	November 2	Israeli forces reach Suez Canal.
	November 4	Soviet army moves into Budapest.
	November 6	Great Britain and France accept cease-fire in Egypt. Eisenhower is reelected.
1957	October 4	Sputnik I is launched by Soviet Union.
1958	July 15	American troops are sent to Lebanon.
1959	January 2	Fidel Castro takes power in Cuba.
	April 15	John Foster Dulles resigns as American secretary of state.
1960	May 1	U2 spy plane is shot down over Soviet Union.
	May 16	Eisenhower-Khrushchev summit is canceled.
1960	January 20	John F. Kennedy is inaugurated as president of the United States.
	April 17	Bay of Pigs invasion of Cuba begins. Defeat comes by April 20, 1961.
	June 3–4	Vienna summit takes place between Kennedy and Khrushchev.
	August 19	Berlin Wall is built.
1962	October 16,	Cuban Missile Crisis begins.
	October 28	Crisis ends when Khrushchev agrees to remove missiles from Cuba.
1963	June 16	Kennedy delivers his "*Ich bin ein Berliner*" speech.
	November 22	Lyndon Johnson becomes president after Kennedy's assassination.
1964	August 7	Gulf of Tonkin Resolution passed in Congress to authorize American military action.
	October 14	Khrushchev is removed from power and replaced by collective leadership. Leonid Brezhnev soon becomes dominant member.
	November 3	Johnson wins reelection.
1965	March 8	First American combat troops arrive in Vietnam.
1967	June 5–10	Six-Day War occurs in Middle East.

1968	Jan 30–Feb 25	Tet Offensive in Vietnam takes place.
	March 31	Johnson announces he will not seek reelection.
	August 21	Soviet and Warsaw Pact troops occupy Prague to crush reforms.
1969	January 20	Richard Nixon becomes president of the United States.
1972	February 21	Nixon goes to China.
1973	January 23	Paris Agreements designed to end Vietnam War are signed.
	October 6–23	War starts between Israel and Egypt and Syria.
1974	August 8	Nixon resigns, replaced by Gerald Ford.
1975	April 30	Saigon falls to North Vietnamese forces.
1977	January 20	Jimmy Carter becomes president of the United States.
1979	January 15	Shah of Iran falls from power.
	March 26	Peace treaty between Egypt and Israel is signed.
	November 4	American embassy in Tehran is seized by Iranian students.
	December 27	Soviets invade Afghanistan.
1981	January 20	Ronald Reagan becomes president of the United States.
1982	November 10	Brezhnev dies.
1983	March 8	Reagan speech introduces term "evil empire."
1985	March 11	Mikhail Gorbachev becomes head of Communist Party.
	November 19–21	First Reagan-Gorbachev summit.
1988	February 8	Gorbachev announces Soviet withdrawal from Afghanistan.
1989	January 20	George H.W. Bush becomes president of the United States.
	June 3	Tiananmen Square massacre occurs in Beijing, China.
	November 9	Berlin Wall falls.
1990	August 2	Iraq invades Kuwait.
1991	February 24	Operation Desert Storm begins.
	August 19	Unsuccessful coup against Gorbachev begins.
	December 25	Gorbachev resigns as president of Soviet Union.

Frontis

1. *Blood, Toil, Tears and Sweat: Winston Churchill's Famous Speeches*, ed., with an introduction by David Cannidine. London: Cassell, 1989, p. 303.
2. Quoted in Steven M. Gillon and Diane B. Kunz, *America During the Cold War*. Fort Worth: Harcourt Brace Jovanovich, 1993, p. v.

Chapter 1

3. Quoted in Brian Crozier, *The Rise and Fall of the Soviet Empire*. Rocklin, Calif.: Forum, an Imprint of Prima Publishing, 1999, p. 178.
4. Quoted in Theodore C. Sorenson, *Kennedy*. New York: Harper and Row, 1965, p. 601.
5. Ibid., p. 600.
6. Quoted in Forrest C. Pogue, "The Struggle for a New Order," in *The Meaning of Yalta*, ed. John C. Snell. Baton Rouge: Louisiana State University Press, 1956, pp. 3–36.
7. James F. Byrnes, *Speaking Frankly*. New York: Harper and Brothers, 1947, p. 22.
8. Ibid., p. 23.
9. Ibid.
10. Don Cook, *Forging the Alliance: NATO, 1945–1950*. New York: Arbor House/William Morrow, 1989, p. 3.
11. Vladislav Zubok and Constantine Pleshkov, *Inside the Kremlin's Cold War: From Stalin to Khrushchev*. Cambridge: Harvard University Press, 1996, p. 26.
12. Quoted in Cook, p. 5.
13. U.S. Department of State, *Foreign Relations of the United States, Diplomatic Papers, The Conferences at Malta and Yalta*. Washington, D.C.: Government Printing Office, 1955, p. 621.
14. Ibid.
15. Quoted in Zubok and Pleskakov, p. 31.
16. Quoted in Zubok and Pleskakov, p. 49.
17. Sir John Colville, *The Fringes of Power: Downing Street Diaries*. London: Norton, 1985, entry for 23 January 1945, p. 555.
18, Zubok and Pleshakov, p. 34.
19. U.S. Department of State, p. 621.
20. Quoted in Cook, p. 8.
21. Byrnes, p. 45.

Chapter 2

22. Quoted in Zubok and Pleshakov, p. 105.
23. Martin Walker, *The Cold War: A History*. New York: Henry Holt and Company, a John Macrae Book, 1993, p. 23.
24. Cyril E. Black, Jonathan E. Helmreich, Paul C. Helmreich, Charles P. Issawi, and A. James McAdams, *Rebirth: A History of Europe Since World War II*. Boulder, Colo.: Westview Press, 1992, p. 40.
25. Robert Hatch McNeal, *Stalin: Man and Ruler*. New York: New York University Press, 1988, p. 2. See also Adam B. Ulam, *Stalin: The Man and His Era*. Boston: Beacon Press, 1989, pp. 264–265.
26. Quoted in Zubok and Pleshakov, p. 13.
27. Anna M. Cienciala, "Soviet Russia and the Western World, 1921–1941," Slavic-Eurasian Studies Web, University of Kansas, <www.slavweb.com/eng/indexl.html>, p. 13.
28. William L. Shirer, *The Rise and Fall of the Third Reich*. New York: Simon and Schuster, 1960, p. 793.
29. Winston S. Churchill, The Second World War: *The Grand Alliance Boston*: Houghton Mifflin Company, the Riverside Press, 1950, p. 451.
30. Quoted in Shirer, p. 831. *Halder Affidavit*, November 22, 1945, NCA, VIII, pp. 645–646. *Nazi Conspiracy and Aggression*, Nuremberg documents.
31. Figures given in J.T. Dykman, *The Soviet Experience in World War Two*. Washington, D.C.: The Eisenhower Institute, 2003.
32. Quoted in Thomas Parrish, *Berlin in the Balance: 1945–1949*. Reading, Mass.: Addison-Wesley, 1998. p. 95.

Chapter 3

33. Quoted in Walker, p. 38.
34. *Time* magazine, February 18, 1946, quoted in Walker, p. 38.
35. Cook, p. 49.
36. Churchill in *Blood, Toil, Tears and Sweat*, p. 303.
37. Ibid., pp. 296–297.
38. Ibid., p. 303.
39. Ibid., p. 306.
40. Quoted in Cook, p. 56.
41. Quoted in Cook, p. 59.
42. Quoted in Cook, p. 61.

43. "X" (George Kennan), "The Sources of Soviet Conduct," *Foreign Affairs*, July 1947, found at <www.historyguide.org>.
44. Walter Lippmann, *The Cold War: A Study in U.S. Foreign Policy*. New York: Harper and Brothers Publishers, 1947, pp. 61–62.
45. Ibid., p. 62.
46. *U.S. News and World Report*, April 18, 1996, interview of George Kennan by David Gergen, found at <www.pbs.org/newshour/gergen/kennan/html>.
47. Harry S Truman, *Memoirs*, Vol. II. Garden City, N.Y.: Doubleday and Company, 1956, p. 106.
48. Quoted in Walker, p. 51.
49. Quoted in Stephen E. Ambrose, *Eisenhower*, Vol. 2: *The President*. New York: Simon and Schuster, p. 380.
50. Quoted in ibid., p. 177.
51. Quoted in William Bragg Ewald, Jr., *Eisenhower the President: Crucial Days: 1951–1960*. Englewood Cliffs, N.J.: Prentice-Hall, 1980, pp. 119–120.
52. Walker, p. 252.
53. Quoted in Christopher Hilton, *The Wall: The People's Story*. Thrupp,. Gloucestershire, U.K.: Sutton Publishing, 2001, quoted pp. 255–256.

Chapter 4

54. Quoted in Cook, p. 88.
55. Quoted in Zubok and Pleshakov, p. 130.
56. Quoted in Cook, p. 114.
57. Quoted in Parrish, p. 31.
58. Quoted in ibid., p. 210.
59. Quoted in ibid., p. 227.
60. Quoted in ibid., p. 228.
61. William H. Tunner, *Over the Hump*. New York: Duell, Sloan, and Pearce, 1964, p. 154.
62. American Enterprise Association, *The Berlin Crisis*. Washington, D.C.: American Enterprise Association, 1961, p. 9.

Chapter 5

63. Quoted in Hilton, p. 1.
64. Quoted in Sorenson, p. 247.
65. Quoted in *American Enterprise*, p. 23. Statement of Dr. Stefan T. Possony, "Analysis of the Khrushchev Speech of January 6, 1961." Hearing before the Subcommittee to Investigate the Administration of the Internal Security Act and Internal Security Laws, Senate Committee on the Judiciary, 87th Congress, 1st Session, June 16, 1961. Washington, D.C.: Government Printing Office, 1961, p. 7.
66. *New York Times*, June 7, 1961, quoted in *American Enterprise*, p. 24.
67. *Orbis*, Summer 1961, pp. 128–129, quoted in *American Enterprise*, p. 25.
68. U.S. government statement of July 17, 1961, quoted in *American Enterprise*, p. 30.
69. Quoted in Walker, p. 157.
70. Quoted in Hilton, p. 13.
71. *New York Times*, July 30, 1961, quoted in *American Enterprise*, p. 31.
72. Cited in Hilton, p. 24.
73. Quoted in ibid., p. 37.
74. Quoted in ibid., pp. 38–39.

Chapter 6

75. Quoted in Cook, p. 166.
76. "Considerations Affecting the Conclusions of a North Atlantic Security Pact," PPS43, November 23, 1948, in *Containment: Documents on American Policy and Strategy, 1945–1950*, ed. Thomas H. Etzold and John Lewis Gaddis. New York: Columbia University Press, 1978, p. 158..
77. Quoted in Cook, p. 185.
78. Quoted in Byrnes, p. 193.

Chapter 7

79. Quoted in Ambrose, pp. 376–377.
80. Michael B. Oren, *Six Days of War*. London: Oxford University Press, 2002, p. 6.
81. Yosef Govrin, *Israeli-Soviet Relations, 1953–1967: From Confrontation to Disruption*. London: Frank Cass, 1990, p. 66.
82. Anthony Nutting, *Nasser*. New York: E.P. Dutton and Company, 1972, p. 1.
83. Quoted in Zubok and Pleshakov, p. 183.
84. Quoted in *Time* magazine, January 7, 1957. Found at <www.historical-textarchive.com>.
85. Dwight David Eisenhower, *Waging Peace*. Garden City, N.Y.: Doubleday and Company, 1965, pp. 94–95.
86. Quoted in Oren, p. 93.
87. Quoted in Oren, p. 92.

Chapter 8

88. Milton Mayer, "The Art of the Impossible," Center for the Study of Democratic Institutions, Occasional Paper, vol. 1, no. 3, April 1969, p. 44.
89. "Prague Defies the Kremlin," *Newsweek*, July 29, 1968, p. 33.
90. Ibid., p. 35.
91. Colin Chapman, *August 21st, The Rape of Czechoslovakia*. New York: J. B. Lippincott, 1968, p. 30.
92. Ibid., p. 33.
93. Ibid., p. 41.

Chapter 9

94. Quoted in Mark Galeotti, Afghanistan: The Soviet Union's Last War. London: Frank Cass, 1990, p. 231.
95. Quoted in Hilton, p. 267.
96. Quoted in ibid., p. 294.
97. Quoted in ibid., p. 295.
98. Quoted in ibid., p. 298.
99. Quoted in ibid.

Ambrose, Stephen E. *Eisenhower, Vol. 2: The President.* New York: Simon and Schuster, 1984.

American Enterprise Association. *The Berlin Crisis.* Washington, D.C.: American Enterprise Association, 1961.

Black, Cyril E., Jonathan E. Helmreich, Paul C. Helmreich, Charles P. Issawi, and A. James McAdams. *Rebirth: A History of Europe Since World War II.* Boulder, Colo.: Westview Press, 1992.

Breitbart, Aaron (Simon Weisenthal Center, Los Angeles). Personal communication (e-mail messages) to author, May 6 and 8, 2003.

Byrnes, James F. *Speaking Frankly.* New York: Harper and Brothers, 1947.

Chapman, Colin *August 21st, The Rape of Czechoslovakia.* New York: J. B. Lippincott, 1968.

Churchill, Winston S. *Blood, Toil, Tears and Sweat: Winston Churchill's Famous Speeches,* edited, with an introduction by David Cannidine. London: Cassell, 1989.

———. *The Second World War: The Grand Alliance.* Boston: Houghton Mifflin Company, the Riverside Press, 1950.

Cienciala, Anna M. "Soviet Russia and the Western World, 1921– 1941," Slavic-Eurasian Studies Web, University of Kansas, <*www.slavweb.com/eng/indexl.html*>.

Colville, Sir John. *The Fringes of Power: Downing Street Diaries.* London: Norton, 1985, entry for 23 January 1945.

"Considerations Affecting the Conclusions of a North Atlantic Security Pact," PPS43, November 23, 1948. *In Containment: Documents on American Policy and Strategy, 1945–1950,* edited by Thomas H. Etzold and John Lewis Gaddis. New York: Columbia University Press, 1978, p. 154.

Cook, Don. *Forging the Alliance: NATO, 1945–1950.* New York: Arbor House/William Morrow, 1989.

Crozier, Brian. *The Rise and Fall of the Soviet Empire.* Rocklin, Calif.: Forum, an Imprint of Prima Publishing, 1999.

Dalleck, R. "The Medical Ordeals of JFK." *The Atlantic Monthly,* December 2002, vol. 290, no. 5, pp. 49–61.

Dykman, J. T. *The Soviet Experience in World War Two.* Washington, D.C.: The Eisenhower Institute, 2003.

Eisenhower, Dwight David. *Waging Peace.* Garden City, N.Y.: Doubleday and Company, 1965.

Ewald, William Bragg, Jr. *Eisenhower the President: Crucial Days: 1951–1960.* Englewood Cliffs, N.J.: Prentice-Hall, 1980.

Gaddis, John Lewis. *We Now Know.* Oxford: Oxford University Press, 1997.

Galeotti, Mark. *Afghanistan: The Soviet Union's Last War.* London: Frank Cass, 1990.

Gergen, David. *U.S. News and World Report,* April 18, 1996, interview of George Kennan by David Gergen, found at <*www.pbs.org/newshour/gergen/kennan/html*>.

Gillon, Steven M., and Diane B. Kunz. *America During the Cold War.* Fort Worth: Harcourt Brace Jovanovich, 1993.

Govrin, Yosef. *Israeli-Soviet Relations, 1953–1967: From Confrontation to Disruption.* London: Frank Cass, 1990.

Hilton, Christopher. *The Wall: The People's Story.* Thrupp,. Gloucestershire, U.K.: Sutton Publishing, 2001.

Kennan, George. *Memoirs: 1925–1963.* Boston: Little, Brown, 1967, 1972.

Kepel, Giles. *Jihad: The Trail of Political Islam.* Translated by Anthony F. Roberts. Cambridge: The Belknap Press of the Harvard University Press, 2002.

Lippmann, Walter. *The Cold War: A Study in U.S. Foreign Policy.* New York: Harper and Brothers, 1947.

Mayer, Martin. "The Art of the Impossible." Center for the Study of Democratic Institutions, Occasional Paper, vol. 1, no. 3, April 1969.

McNeal, Robert Hatch. *Stalin: Man and Ruler.* New York: New York University Press, 1988.

Nutting, Anthony. *Nasser.* New York: E. P. Dutton and Company, 1972.

Oren, Michael B. *Six Days of War.* London: Oxford University Press, 2002.

Parrish, Thomas. *Berlin in the Balance: 1945–1949.* Reading, Mass.: Addison-Wesley, 1998.

Pogue, Forrest C. "The Struggle for a New Order." In *The Meaning of Yalta*, edited by John C. Snell. Baton Rouge: Louisiana State University Press, 1956, pp. 3–36.

"Prague Defies the Kremlin." *Newsweek,* July 29, 1968.

Shirer, William L. *The Rise and Fall of the Third Reich.* New York: Simon and Schuster, 1960.

Sorenson, Theodore C. *Kennedy.* New York: Harper and Row, 1965.

Time magazine, January 7, 1957. Found at <*www.historicaltextarchive.com*>.

Truman, Harry S, *Memoirs,* vol. II. Garden City, N.Y.; Doubleday and Company, 1956.

Tunner, William H. *Over the Hump.* New York: Duell, Sloan, and Pearce, 1964.

Tusa, Ann. *The Last Division: A History of Berlin, 1945–1989.* Reading, Mass.: Addison-Wesley, 1997.

Ulam, Adam B. *Stalin: The Man and His Era.* Boston: Beacon Press, 1989.

U.S. Department of State. *Foreign Relations of the United States, Diplomatic Papers, The Conferences at Malta and Yalta.* Washington, D.C.: Government Printing Office, 1955.

Walker, Martin. *The Cold War: A History.* New York: Henry Holt and Company, a John Macrae Book, 1993.

"X" (George Kennan). "The Sources of Soviet Conduct." *Foreign Affairs,* July 1947, found at <*www.historyguide.org*>.

Zubok, Vladimir, and Constantine Pleshakov. *Inside the Kremlin's Cold War: From Stalin to Khrushchev.* Cambridge: Harvard University Press, 1996.

Association of the United States Army. *1989: End of a Decade–End of An Era*. Special Report. Arlington, Va.: Association of the United States Army, 1990.

Gaddis, John Lewis. *Russia, the Soviet Union, and the United States: An Interpretive History*. New York: McGraw-Hill, 1990.

Gelb, Norman *The Berlin Wall*. London: Joseph, 1986.

Harbutt, Fraser J. *The Iron Curtain: Churchill, America, and the Origins of the Cold War*. New York: Oxford University Press, 1986.

LaFeber, Walter. *America, Russia, and the Cold War: 1945–1971*. 2d ed. New York: John Wiley and Sons, 1967, 1977.

Lesch, David W. *1979: The Year that Shaped the Modern Middle East*. Boulder, Colo.: Westview Press, 2001.

Lukas, John. *1945—Year Zero*. Garden City, N.Y.: Doubleday, 1978.

Stiftung, Hans Bockler. *The 10th Anniversary of the Fall of the Berlin Wall*. Baden-Baden, Germany: Nomos, 1999.

Sulzberger, C.L. *Such a Peace: The Roots and Ashes of Yalta*. New York: Continuum, 1982.

Varsoni, Antonio, and Elena Calandri. *The Failure of Peace in Europe, 1943–48*. New York: Palgrave, 2002.

page:

Bruce L. Brager has worked for many years as both a staff and a freelance writer-editor, specializing in history, political science, foreign policy, energy, and defense and military topics. *The Iron Curtain* is his fifth book. His previous book for Chelsea House, *The Monitor Versus the Merrimack* (Chelsea House Publishers, July 2003), tells the story of the influential naval battle, the first between ironclad vessels, from the American Civil War. Brager has published more than 50 articles for the general and specialized history markets. He was raised in the Washington, D.C., area and in New York City. He graduated from the George Washington University and currently lives in Arlington, Virginia.

George J. Mitchell served as chairman of the peace negotiations in Northern Ireland during the 1990s. Under his leadership, an historic accord, ending decades of conflict, was agreed to by the governments of Ireland and the United Kingdom and the political parties in Northern Ireland. In May 1998, the agreement was overwhelmingly endorsed by a referendum of the voters of Ireland, North and South. Senator Mitchell's leadership earned him worldwide praise and a Nobel Peace Prize nomination. He accepted his appointment to the U.S. Senate in 1980. After leaving the Senate, Senator Mitchell joined the Washington, D.C. law firm of Piper Rudnick, where he now practices law. Senator Mitchell's life and career have embodied a deep commitment to public service and he continues to be active in worldwide peace and disarmament efforts.

James I. Matray is professor of history and chair at California State University, Chico. He has published more than forty articles and book chapters on U.S.-Korean relations during and after World War II. Author of *The Reluctant Crusade: American Foreign Policy in Korea, 1941–1950 and Japan's Emergence as a Global Power*, his most recent publication is *East Asia and the United States: An Encyclopledia of Relations Since 1784*. Matray also is international columnist for the *Donga Iibo* in South Korea.